AF317050

Through These Eyes

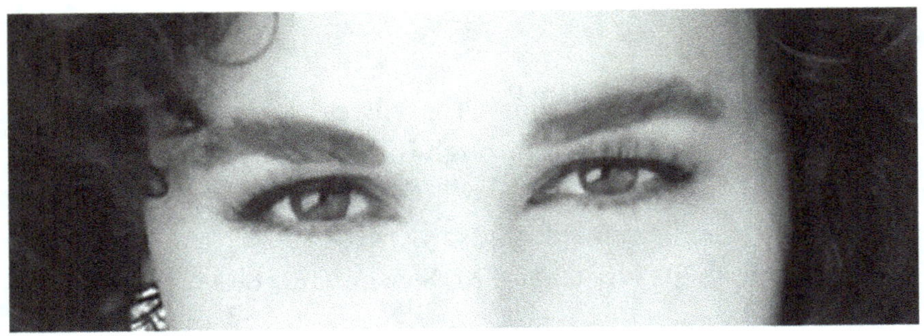

Behind the Scenes of Makeup Artist LuAnn Mancini

Her Journey and Relationships with the Powerful

a memoir

Cherie Swisher and LuAnn Mancini

Through These Eyes

by Cherie Swisher and LuAnn Mancini

As a self-made makeup artist, LuAnn Mancini built a business and a career from the ground up—and with it, crossed paths with some of the most influential and impactful people of her day. Through this thirty-five-year journey, living and working in Fort Worth, Texas, she serendipitously found herself among the rich and powerful. Her work included meeting and working with Dan Rather and politicians such as George W. Bush, Bill and Hillary Clinton, Laura Bush, Ross Perot, Lady Bird Johnson, Vladimir Putin, and Mikhail Gorbachev. Her work with celebrities included Gretchen Carlson, Andrew Llyod Webber, Van Cliburn, Joan Rivers, and the Dallas Cowboys Cheerleaders. She was behind the scenes and witnessed history in the making during the student protests in Tiananmen Square; the Oklahoma City bombing; the Columbine shooting; the Discovery Launch with John Glenn; the death of James Byrd Jr. in Jasper, Texas; Hurricane Georges; and World Youth Day. Her work settings included Air Force I, CBS News, Cape Canaveral, Tiananmen Square, Moscow, and the jail cell of Jasper, Texas.

Throughout this time, she perfected the LuAnn Mancini line of cosmetics, created the LuAnn Mancini Studio dealing almost exclusively in makeup, and crafted one of the first airbrushes in the cosmetics industry.

Journey with her, *Through These Eyes*, from behind the scenes and listen to stories artfully woven.

To my daughter, Shannon,
who keeps me grounded, the reason for my
being, and the center of my world.

Table of Contents

Authors' Notes

"This is my take on it"

As I look back over a very rewarding career, I am left with many fond memories, notes and letters, souvenirs and trinkets, and photographs. When I began this journey over thirty-five years ago, I had no idea how far it would take me, and I made no attempt to record dates, times, and specific details. I am speaking from the heart, with pride, to share this journey with you—and I hope that you will forgive any discrepancies with history.

LuAnn Mancini

If you have ever met LuAnn or may someday have the pleasure of meeting her, you will meet an excitable, distracted, joyful, scattered, effervescent spirit. She is a ping pong ball in action. In the retelling of her stories to me, this was never clearer. In my writing of her stories to you, the reader, I made the conscious and intentional decision to retain what I will call tense skipping, changing from past tense to present tense frequently, to preserve her voice. It is one of many things which makes her unusual journey even more amazing, to channel this energy in an unpredictable profession into a success story. I hope you will enjoy getting to know her.

Cherie Swisher
Her loving sister

Prologue

"Earliest Beginnings"

Poverty teaches you a lot of things; among them, creativity, perseverance, and resilience. What you don't have, you create. What you want to get from life, you struggle for. When you fail, you get back up.

I knew at the early age of ten years old that I wanted to be an artist. I desperately wanted to paint and did not have paint, brushes, or even paper. Instead, a brown paper bag torn open as my canvas, berries and dirt as my palette, and twigs as my paintbrush were my tools to create. What I did not know at this early age was that my medium as an adult would not be clay, watercolors, or charcoal. My art form was makeup. Self-taught, as I learned the same principles of the great artists—contour, shape, texture, proportion. I was able to meet some of the most influential people of our time. I worked behind the curtain and looked into their private world.

Tiananmen Square; Beijing, China - May 1989
"History Unfolding"

The choppers came from out of nowhere. At first there was just one, then more and more. They looked like a swarm of giant bugs hovering above us, descending on the flatbed truck. The bodies of the eight helicopters were camouflage and dark in color, sent from the Communist Chinese Party to disperse the previously peaceful protesters. The immense blades were casting dirt and gravel, and the sound was deafening.

The television crew was on the flatbed truck—an attempt to separate us from the thousands of people in the streets. A journalist sat cross-legged on the truck, with a typewriter and makeshift desk on his lap. The Communist Party was about to declare martial law, and any communications to the rest of the world would be blocked. He furiously tapped away at the story, racing against the clock. The sound and tech crew were left to fend for themselves, gathering equipment amidst the chaos.

I watched the crowd in their drab colors begin to flee, an ocean of movement beginning to build like a tidal wave. The numbers had grown over the past few weeks to over a million, and it was more than the government was willing to tolerate.

As the scene began to escalate, Dan yelled at us, "Get to the car!" I grabbed my makeup bag, and we began to scramble toward the vehicle as if our lives depended on it. And they did. The driver and car were within view, and we somehow managed to find our way amidst the turbulent winds. "Soak your towels in water and be prepared to cover your faces! They may use chemical warfare! Get on the floor of the car."

If you're asking yourself, how did I find myself in this scenario, I look back and ask the same question. It began as a simple love, creating with color and texture and always having a vision. Rewind with me over the past thirty-five years, where I oftentimes found myself in implausible and improbable circumstances.

The Burden of Childhood - 1960s

"From Fairy Tale to Food Stamps"

I sat with my head on top of my folded arms, on the table of my school desk, sobbing uncontrollably. The teachers did not know what to do with me. It was a large classroom of students in a neighborhood public school, and they had over thirty other fourth grade students to contend with. I was dressed in a plaid school dress, with my bare legs exposed to the elements of winter. Girls were not allowed to wear pants at school. My legs were thin, sores on my body did not heal quickly, and I was probably undernourished. I owned one pair of shoes.

There was no point in looking into my lunch bag to see what I would have for lunch. It would be a peanut butter and jelly sandwich. My mother always reminded me to bring home the brown paper sack so it could be reused for the next day's lunch. Ziploc bags were an extravagance. We would use the plastic bread bag for chips. I envied the lunch boxes that the other children carried.

I lay in the nurse's office, unable to coexist in the classroom, until 2:00 p.m., when I would be allowed to go home. Home. My current home. My temporary home.

I was born into a blue-collar Italian family in 1956. My three older brothers preceded my arrival, and my parents were thrilled to now have a daughter to welcome into the family. We ate meals together, went to Catholic mass, and I attended catechism regularly. Our Sunday meal would be a beef pot roast, surrounded by peeled potatoes, carrots, celery, and onion. If I pushed the vegetables around the plate long enough, I could get away without eating them.

I always felt like a princess, even after the arrival of my three younger siblings. I could go to the swimming pool on hot summer days, ride in the golf cart with my father, and if things went my way, I would get to purchase candy from the pro shop after a day on the golf course. My favorite treat was the hard, pastel candy necklace on the elastic string that would leave a sticky residue on my neck. If I finished it before I got home, no one would be the wiser.

I lived in a world of love and adoration from my father, my grandmother, and my siblings—but most of all, from my mother. It was a world that would be shattered a few short years later, when I found myself living with my aunt and uncle, my two cousins, and my younger sister and older brother, separated from the nucleus of what I knew to be home.

Our circumstances found our family in five different homes, evicted from the security of our brick house and separate bedrooms. My mother and father would no longer be living under the same roof, and my siblings would go to different homes while my family "could get on our feet."

The loving support of my extended family and relatives was what kept us from becoming homeless, but it was not home. I was not surrounded by my best friends—my siblings—and we would not be sitting down together as a family for beef pot roast on Sundays.

I began having dreams at night, or I should say "a dream." A recurring, repetitive vignette into my subconscious of what I had lost. Only years later did I come to understand the underlying meaning. The dream was of a hardboiled egg, a cracked shell with fraying edges. I tried desperately to slice the egg into equal portions, taking great care not to damage its contents. As hard as I struggled to measure and calculate the ingredients into creating a souffle of my former life, the egg was cracked.

We sat in my aunt's automobile, my three younger siblings and I, on the street outside of what would be our new home. The building was a small three-bedroom, one-bath, wood framed house in a struggling neighborhood, with a small front and backyard and a detached garage. A massive evergreen tree engulfed the front yard—the original owners of the home not having the foresight to recognize that it would dwarf the house in years to come. The overgrown shrubbery in front of the home obscured the small front porch, with its decaying concrete and protruding screen door.

My siblings watched from across the street as my mother and I crossed the threshold and stepped through the front entry to tour the home with my aunt, all the while trying not to let us see her despair. It was badly unkempt, with dated features, musty carpet odors, and the remains of a large mound of butter left in the single toilet bowl.

My extended family was not wealthy, not even well to do, yet they were stable. Because of their strong family bonds to each other, they rallied to purchase the small home on Julian Circle and rented it to my mother for below market rates. The home would be a new place to start, a new beginning, albeit meager.

One day, a 1956 Ford Mercury Monterey appeared on our driveway, alongside the back stoop, and parked in front of the one-car garage. The Merc-O-Matic, or "The Beast," as we called it, was not new by any stretch of the imagination, but it was new to us. It was recognizable by its crimson body and black top, ornamented with considerable amounts of weathered chrome. The Beast, although worn and tired, allowed my mother to drive to the grocery store, church, and work, rather than take public transit, and we were no longer confined to the one square block of our neighborhood.

I recall my mother speaking of standing in line to purchase food stamps, how demeaning it was to her, and that she'd never envisioned herself being in this position. She would work hard and strive to be able to purchase enough food for our family without government assistance, to be able to shed the overt label of poverty while in the grocery store.

It was a harrowing period in my young life. We were latchkey kids. At times strangers would visit our home, the men in business suits and the women in dresses and coordinating pump shoes, with my mother always making sure that the house was in order and that we looked presentable. At the time I did not understand why these visitors were so important.

I became the caregiver of my two-year-old brother, as best an eleven-year-old could. He would come to me in desperation, his dark brown eyes and long lashes filled with tears, because his teeth were in pain. He had not been to a dentist, and the decay in his teeth would cause agony anytime that he would eat. I would retrieve his toothbrush from the bathroom and scrub and massage his tooth until the pain subsided. Oftentimes he came to me, still in diapers, tormented by diaper rash, yet holding the tube of Desitin for me to help him.

Once we began attending the local public school, I was responsible for picking him up from the neighbor's house and walking him home. As my younger siblings and I left home in the mornings to walk ourselves to school, he would stand at the large picture window on the front of our house, his tears running down his cheeks as we walked away. When we returned after a school day to pick him up at daycare, he was ever so glad to be reunited with his three older sisters.

My mother scrimped and saved to buy my younger sister a new bicycle for her birthday. It was a royal blue Schwinn with a white banana seat and translucent handles that glistened and reflected the sunlight. The tassels hanging from the handlebars moved with the breeze. She would let me ride it, and one day I asked to borrow it to ride to the strip mall a few blocks away. She had only had the bike for a few weeks but was always willing to share.

Riding by myself through the back streets of our neighborhood to Hested's, the local department store, I then parked the bicycle at the back entrance to the store. It would only be a few minutes that I would be in the store; surely it would be fine. I parked the bike in the bicycle rack just a few feet away from the double glass doors and went inside to spend my allowance.

When I came out of the store, I was in disbelief. The bicycle was gone. My sister's birthday present had vanished. It was a neighborhood that invited theft. I began to panic and ran to the Big Top convenience store next door. I pleaded and begged with the man behind the cash register to help me call the police, but he was unwilling. I ran home, breathless and in tears, my words spewing out between gasps of air. I looked at my sister with remorse, begging forgiveness, hoping she would understand. She looked up at me and replied very simply, "It's gone. There's nothing we can do about it." In our world, we were taught that when something broke or was worn out, it could not be replaced. There was no money. We simply had to do without.

At one point, my elderly grandmother came to live with us. My lasting memory was of her lying bedridden and in pain from hip surgery. When I would come home from elementary school, she would ask me to help her with the bedpan and to help her bathe. On one such day after cleaning her up, she reached down and pulled a diamond ring with side set stones from her small, frail hand and placed it into the palm of my hand. She wrapped her fingers, weathered by time, around my hand. Her wedding ring from Italy was the only way she could express her gratitude.

We became the target of bullying from the older neighborhood children. One day our pet rabbit was found dead in the garage, killed by a bullet from a BB gun. My three younger siblings and I ran into the house, screaming and in tears, traumatized by the sight of our dead pet.

A young girl in the neighborhood confided in me that her older brothers were "practicing" kissing her, so they would know what to do when they began dating. At eleven years old, I didn't fully understand the implications of this personal information. As she confided in me more and more about her family situation, I knew there was something very wrong.

Living in this new environment brought with it many changes, risks, and temptations. I grew up very quickly, desperately wanting to fit in. We teetered on survival and the precipice of bad decisions. I was in sixth grade, hoping to find my tribe, my seat at the table. When I entered junior high, the school was one of the largest within the school district, and it was at the peak of racial tensions and forced school bussing within the 1960s. I considered myself lucky that I did not have to ride the school bus and endure the bullying. It was easier to tolerate the one mile walk to the junior high.

Students without a lot of support often slipped between the cracks. The popular kids were the tough kids, the leaders oftentimes going down the wrong path. We began to hang out, the good girl running with the bad kids. I was the one they labeled "Goody Two Shoes." I went to school dreading my academic classes but passionate about art and PE, and they spent their days skipping school and breaking into homes.

One afternoon after school, I walked into the home of one of my new friends to a living room filled with jewelry, sterling candelabras, money, and pornography photographs, my eyes wide in amazement. A bedsheet was spread out on the floor to display the bounty and was also used as a knapsack to bundle the treasures and hoist them over a shoulder.

"Where did you get all of this stuff?" I asked in bewilderment.

"This is our loot from today." It was their haul from their day of break-ins and evading the police.

"If you want to go with us, we're going again tomorrow."

Despite the devastating circumstances of our home life and lack of financial security, I recognized that this would lead to no good. It was then that I knew I had to find a new circle of friends. For this I must thank my mother for instilling in me the sense to know when to walk away. The foundation to know right from wrong. It did not matter that I had none of this—the end did not justify the means.

In May of 1989, I found myself in Beijing, China, amidst the poverty and during the events and troubling times of Tiananmen Square. I am brought back to the burden of my childhood and recall feeling compassion and empathy for the citizens on the streets, but mostly a feeling of hopelessness and anguish, uncertain as to what their destiny might be, with no promising future in sight.

Serendipity - 1985

"The Most Unlikely of Circumstances"

It was the unlikeliest of places, a conference for realtors in Las Vegas, Nevada. The hotel was large and nondescript. Ballrooms were filled with tables arranged in pedantic rows, skirting to the floor. There were displays and charts on aluminum tripods, illuminated by fluorescent lighting overhead. Business cards and bowls of candy to entice people into the lecture halls were neatly displayed.

I offhandedly looked on with my husband, chatting to pass the time. It was going to be a long couple of days. Real estate did not inspire my creativity. I smiled as he greeted people and shared portfolios.

My work was gratifying. Makeup, to many, might not seem like a career, but the "elite" had a busy lifestyle. Fashion models on set, debutante balls and weddings, pageant contestants, and dermatology patients filled my appointment calendar. I was becoming well known in the Fort Worth area, and my studio, now in its third year, was doing well. I had two makeup artists under my watchful eye; I was fulfilling my dreams.

I never liked school. I was not a traditional student. To be able to achieve my goals in the makeup industry was what many would consider fruitless.

I wandered over to the table, curiously looking around and striking up a conversation. She, too, had some connection to the real estate world. We talked to help fill the time of "hurry up and wait." We connected, and at some point, I think we even slipped away to play a few hands of blackjack. I shared my profession with her and told her about myself.

If you look back over your life and say, that one person, that one incident, that one event changed the trajectory of my life, I would say this was it. She said, "My husband, Wayne Nelson, is bureau chief with CBS in Dallas. Because they predominantly do news, they don't need makeup very often, but let me pass along your business card."

I did not, in fact, hear anything for a very long time. It was a wishful thought, maybe a pot of gold at the end of that ever-elusive rainbow. To be quite truthful, I had forgotten about meeting this young woman at the conference. It was a good year before the phone would ring, that CBS called to book me. I was asked to be on location for an interview. I was thrilled that even after this much time had transpired, my contact would come through. I cleared my calendar, stocked, checked, and rechecked my travel kit, only to have the client cancel at the last minute. *Well,* I thought, *at least they have my business card in their Rolodex.*

A few more months passed, and I again got "the call." This was an interview with a prestigious senator. As I anxiously awaited the upcoming date, I later got a second call to cancel.

"He refuses to wear makeup. Thank you for your time."

It is now January of 1988. Karma had me in its sights, because the third time was the charm. This was a big one. "Dan Rather is coming to Dallas for the 20th anniversary of the John F. Kennedy assassination. He'll be shooting the evening news, live, on Friday, and needs a makeup artist."

I couldn't have anticipated being more excited, no more than I could have anticipated the ice storm that was on its way through Dallas. Many cities have snowplows, salt trucks, and equipment to handle this kind of weather, but this was Texas. There was black ice at the D/FW Airport, the storm lasted five days, and nobody was out on the streets.

I was scheduled to be in Dallas at 2:00 p.m. on a Friday for the 5:00 p.m. evening news. Typically, this would have been a one-hour drive, even in heavy traffic!

"Get on the road at 7:00 a.m." The roads were covered with shards of ice, resembling boulders of rock candy from a confectioner's shop. Texans refer to this as "cobblestone ice."

I loaded up my little white Prelude and headed east, inching along. At times I was able to go just 5–10 miles an hour. The ice was so bumpy and jagged I thought I would surely puncture a tire. I should have had chains. Without meaning to sound redundant, this was Texas, and there was no need for chains!

The trip took me about three and a half hours to get to Dallas from Fort Worth. I arrived at about 11:00 or 11:30 a.m. The crew was relieved to see me, but only half as relieved as I was to get there. I could now exhale and set up my workspace, only to wait for a few hours more.

As I looked around and took in the scene, I thought that this was my break. This was a big deal for me, to do their main anchor, evening news, live. *What if I get something in his contact? Is this going to be good enough? Will I be able to go in and not create any obstacles?*

I was introduced to Mr. Rather and went to work. If I was only getting one shot at this, it had to be perfect. The big guns from CBS were on location. Mission accomplished, or so I thought. Dan was in place under the bright lights, and the executive producer called me into the control room to check my work on the monitor. When I looked on screen, I immediately flinched.

He has white rings under his eyes. Neutralize the concealer. He's over-highlighted.

I overdid it; it was too heavy-handed. I needed to dial it back. I had to quickly step back in and make a few changes. They smiled knowingly and knew that I had caught my own mistakes.

The news went live, broadcast across the whole nation. Don't dare cough, don't dare sneeze. With commercials and the excitement of the moment, thirty minutes goes by quickly. The broadcast was done, and I felt honored to have been hired, not knowing whether there would be another opportunity.

As I'm packing up my kit, Dan says to me, "You'll be back tomorrow, right?" I'm nodding yes, and I'm thinking no, as I'm looking to the producer. *"No, I'm not. I have ten appointments tomorrow!"*

How do you turn down this chance? Is any one client more important than another? I had to graciously reschedule my other clients, yet when I explained the situation to my clients, they were all very proud of me and happy to reschedule. My clients were loyal. Dan never knew I had to move my whole day; he never would have asked that of me. It was a once in a lifetime shot, and I had to make it happen.

By the second day, I was already more comfortable with the crew and no longer nervous to be around them. The weather had already begun to clear, and the drive was not as treacherous as the previous day. We were going to film the "first-ever" episode of *48 Hours*. As I'm sitting on an equipment trunk eating lunch, it felt like family.

We were at the Parkland Hospital in Dallas for the 20th anniversary of the assassination of President John F. Kennedy. As Dan interviewed the doctors, he artfully wove the story together. It was a wonderful workday. I felt so accomplished. It was my first job with CBS. I had no idea that China, Russia, Japan, dignitaries, celebrities, politicians, and astronauts would follow, down the road.

Again, I left thinking, *A feather in my cap. It will be good for local business. And it pays well!* I was riding high. To tell you the truth, adrenaline can carry you for days. It's a good thing; I had to make the trip back. *No snow tires. I should have had chains.*

---

48 Hours episode
https://danratherjournalist.org/
investigative-journalist/48-hours/48-hours-hospital

The Neighborhood - 1966

"A Very Short Life"

Pop! Pop! Pop! I stopped short, questioning what I was hearing. Had I really just heard gunshots, or was that the sound of a car backfiring? This was not the world I was accustomed to, not the world I knew. You work hard, try to get good grades in school, and clean your plate at the dinner table. If you were good, Santa Claus and the Easter Bunny would visit.

I had just rounded the corner of the house from the backyard, climbed the three short steps onto the back stoop, and entered our home through the back screen door. My three younger siblings were inside, seemingly unaware of any danger.

The family room was located at the back of our home, adjacent to the backyard. Tall, wooden cupboards in a natural-colored pine lined the northern wall. A large, braided oval rug lay on the bare floor. An overstuffed sofa sat underneath the picture window overlooking the backyard.

I climbed onto the sofa to peer out of the large window and saw two uniformed policemen in their dark colors. Standing in the yard next to ours, they looked down upon a body, which lay motionless on the hard concrete. There was a pool of red blood on the ice beneath the corpse, surrounded by a sea of white snow. Spent bullets were embedded in the wood trim surrounding the doorway to the detached garage.

We were not to call my mother at work unless it was an emergency. Her employers did not look fondly upon her receiving personal phone calls during the workday. I felt like this might be an emergency.

"Close the drapes and stay away from the window," she said. She would be home early evening, after her shift. She could not risk losing her job that paid $1.40 an hour.

I don't recall the sound of sirens or seeing an ambulance. It was too late. He was a young man, one of two, running from the police. There had been a break-in, a crime in progress, and the authorities were called. The suspects hopped over the short chain-link fences and shrubs that separated the yards. Shots were fired, and shots were returned.

The young boy of nineteen years old lay on the cold ground for what seemed like hours for the investigation to take place, playing out like an episode from *NCIS*. I thought back to my recent past, learning of my friends breaking into houses, wondering whether this was one of their older brothers.

As a grown woman and now a mother, I can only envision this close brush with danger, the possibility of my daughter being struck by a stray bullet. Worse yet, getting that phone call from the police, describing the unimaginable loss of my child. It was a very short life lost for monetary gain of a young man who slipped through the cracks.

Discovery - "Return to Flight" Mission - 1987

"Honorable Men"

On January 28, 1986, the space shuttle Challenger exploded. It was a breathtaking, shocking, and horrific event in the history of our country. Just over a year later, NASA was already underway and planning its next mission. I had the honor of being asked back by CBS to work on location in Houston. The launch of the Discovery was in its final stages.

The shoot was to take place at the Lyndon B. Johnson Space Center, where the five astronauts train and research takes place. The drive from Fort Worth to Houston is typically a four-hour drive; the safe thing to do was to drive down the night before the shoot.

We met in a large hangar with the rest of the team. In the late '80s, the space program was still very much a male-dominated profession. I was "one of the guys." Although I was there primarily as Dan Rather's "hair and makeup," it is a very common practice to ask the interviewees if they would like makeup. Dan thanked me for my work and then off-handedly said, "Don't get your feelings hurt. They're not going to want makeup. Don't be surprised if they don't accept."

I walked into the room and introduced myself simply as "Makeup. Would anyone like to be touched up?" Standing before me were the five astronauts: Commander Frederick H. "Rick" Hauck; Pilot Richard O. Covey; and Mission Specialists, David C. Hilmers, John M. "Mike" Lounge, and George D. "Pinky" Nelson. I later came to learn that this was "not their first rodeo." All five of the astronauts had launched into space before and were part of the frequent flyer program.

If I were to describe these men to you in a few words, I would say tidy, fit, crisp, clean-cut, centered, and focused. They were not afraid. They were the right-stuff kind of guys. Anyone would say so! They were dressed in what I will call a "jumpsuit," with the NASA logo on the uniform.

The room went silent. At the time I didn't know who was in charge. I can say with confidence that makeup was not a common occurrence in the space program. In a studio setting, on a stage or in a theater, certainly, but not here.

Quickly thereafter, Commander Hauck said, "I'll go first. I never ask my men to do something I wouldn't do first." An honorable man, first and foremost.

I smiled to myself as he hopped up onto the corner of a desk. It took me no more than twenty minutes for all five men. I take a lot of pride when applying makeup to a male. If you look on-screen, no one should notice that they are wearing makeup, just a more handsome, less-flawed, healthier version of themselves. I like to say that I'm erasing some of the markings of time. There was no mirror. I was their mirror. These were not vain men, and they had to have trust in me. It's a nice way to work. There was no tug of war.

As I left the room, I had a big smile on my face. I felt like I had achieved something. Dan looked at me quizzically, slightly surprised that they hadn't waved me off with the gesture of an arm. Having done hundreds of high-profile interviews, he's not a guy who surprises easily. He had a nice smile. No words were exchanged, but he nodded in approval.

I had excitedly accepted the invitation to join the team for a tour of the facility following the shoot. I tried to capture the moment in my mind, realizing that I was experiencing something that many could not. Although cell phones were invented as early as 1973, they were not commonplace. I could not take a video, and I did not have my camera with me. The tour included artifacts from earlier research and launches, machines, and robots. As we moved through the museum, I was struck by the primitive nature of the equipment, the oversized hand-held telephones. I was in astonishment, thinking to myself that it reminded me of a kindergarten playroom with oversized props. How had we put the lives of astronauts at risk with such immature technology?

I left that day with both sadness and joy. Sadness that it was over, and joy that I had been a part of it. It had happened so quickly. I thought to myself, *Wow. Did that just happen? That's the biggest I'll ever get.*

I was living in Fort Worth. My first contact with CBS for Dan Rather was in Dallas; my second for this interview was in Houston. My work would certainly be contained to Texas. I was the local girl.

Cape Canaveral - 1988

"Return to Flight"

What I didn't know as I left the facility that day was that I would be asked back again. It was the beginning of so much more to come. I didn't know at the time that I would be watching the Discovery launch a year later, September 29, 1988, from the Kennedy Space Center in Florida. Fast forward, again I had the honor of working with Dan Rather for this momentous event.

People were lining the freeway in motorhomes and cars days before, so they could put themselves in a position to watch. CBS had to helicopter Dan in to assure he could get through traffic. They could not risk that he would be delayed, with the throngs of people who were gathering. The rest of the crew was bussed in at 4:00 a.m. to get to Cape Canaveral. When Dan arrived an hour later, and he walked onto the set, it was all systems go.

As I am at Cape Canaveral, I look around me. From this vantage point, at first glance, the launch pad appears as only a speck in the distance. The room is filled with tension. You could feel it in the air. What most people would call a disaster—the explosion of the Challenger space shuttle, fatally killing all on board—had happened just over two years earlier. This launch was now referred to as, "The Return to Flight." But in addition to apprehension, the room was also filled with hope, as we watched these brave men willing to risk their lives.

We were powered up and ready for the prelaunch interview. All the networks were there to film. There were swarms of TV cameras.

A two-story structure was built on stilts to house equipment on the ground level; the broadcast room with a large picture window on the raised portion; and the cameras were on the roof, for a bird's-eye view of the launch. There was a flight of steps leading up the outside of the structure.

Inside of this modular unit was a small workspace and a few offices. There was a very large picture window to see the rocket. I thought back to the space center in Houston, again in amazement at what I was seeing. The progress over the few short years—the things at the museum versus what I was seeing now—it was as if it were two different worlds.

It was Florida, and the humidity was high. A team of men kept cleaning the condensation from the windows. Clean, five seconds would pass, the windows would fog again, repeat.

The countdown began. Like a well-synchronized machine, the tech crew made their last pass at the windows. The cameras switched from viewing Dan Rather to the shuttle, and NASA took over. In a calm but commanding voice, almost as if in slow motion, "FIVE. FOUR. THREE. TWO. ONE. ZERO. AND LIFT-OFF."

We were just five miles from the launch pad, the best view in the house. That poor little girl that didn't have watercolors now has a bird's-eye view. I couldn't have imagined such a life-changing event.

It was so powerful. I don't know how all of Florida didn't rumble. Five miles away, you could feel the vibration in your body. I could only imagine what it felt like to the men on board. If I could feel and hear it rumbling, what it must have felt like to them.

To know what man had created had become so spiritual to me. It became so emotional, something could have happened to them, but they were not afraid.

I was praying and crying at the same time, watching the shuttle liftoff. It brought me to my knees, both physically and emotionally. As the shuttle made its ascent, the people in the room all slowly lowered themselves to see the last trailing image of the shuttle through the picture window and leave our world. It was as if they were all choreographed, moving as one.

I couldn't even speak. I didn't expect it to have that impact on me. To see something of that magnitude that close, to see the flames and power, slow motion, watched it, watched it, it was gone. It took, I'm guessing, sixty seconds, before we couldn't see it anymore. It was a great sense of relief that there was not another tragic explosion. All were on pins and needles.

We all wanted to cheer, but we were still live. Dan was still reporting. You pray you don't have to cough or sneeze; the whole room turns around to look at you! I can only imagine that there was thunderous applause on the freeway. And although there was no clapping or cheering on the set, there was a great sense of relief and exhilaration.

Despite the Challenger tragedy, I know they would all do it again. They had such a love for what they were doing. After having met and worked on these young men, it felt so personal when I watched the shuttle go up, and ever-so-grateful when they returned.

All of these events made makeup intelligent. It felt more intelligent. It didn't have anything to do with personal beauty or glamour; it wasn't about makeup. It was a project, in their area of expertise, and we became one and produced these projects. It felt like I was being challenged.

A week later, I received a photograph of the shuttle launch from the producer of CBS. As I opened the manilla envelope, I smiled to myself, filled with emotion. Deep inside, I knew that I was a small part of history being made.

John Glenn

"Quiet Confidence"

As a private contractor with CBS, I never knew when my phone would ring. NASA continued to study the effects of the aging process on the human body, and who better to take this journey than John Glenn?

"Can you be in Houston?"

One of the first men to orbit the Earth, the astronaut on the Friendship 7, February 20, 1962, the senator… *Let me check my calendar.* Another honor I never thought would come my way.

"Yes, I think I can clear my schedule."

We were at the Lyndon B. Johnson Space Center in Houston. I was directed to a park bench located between two buildings, where he was seated and waiting for me. He was seventy-seven years old and unassumingly blended into the landscape.

As I applied a light makeup to this American hero, he sat quietly, stoic and confident. Vitamin E on his lips, powder to his face, checked his hair, brushed his eyebrows. His piercing blue eyes must have seen so much. Did they ever see fear? As I tried to read his expressions, he was understated. *Why the fuss? This is a mission. I know what my purpose is. I am honored to again serve my country.*

I stand back, watching the interview unfold and conclude, wondering how I would feel if he were a member of my family. Would I be able to sleep at night, knowing the risks he was taking on this perilous flight? Would I be able to endure the uncertainty if he were my father, my husband, or my son? Had this mission ended as tragically as the Challenger, would my knees buckle as I fell to the ground? On this day, I leave thinking, it is not the event that is memorable, it is the man.

Cape Canaveral - 1998

"Time Repeats Itself"

On October 29, 1998, the space shuttle orbiter Discovery launched into space. John Glenn again had the privilege and honor to be aboard.

CBS contracted me to be on sight for this launch. As I settled into my routine, it was "somewhat" comforting to see familiar faces, the stilted set, and a building I was familiar with.

Technology, screens, and the layout of the room had advanced, and the equipment was much more streamlined.

I set out my airbrush, foundation, powder—my palette and tools. Dan Rather greets me, ready to work. I quickly apply makeup to his now familiar features and ready myself to complete his hair. His thick, wavy hair embraced the Florida humidity; nothing a little hairspray can't fix. As I test my non-aerosol hairspray bottle, I quickly realize that the pump is clogged. Anyone who has ever used hairspray has shared this experience at some time. It's almost like asking a toddler to perform for an appreciative audience of aunties. Under pressure, no can do!

With time running tight, I could feel my pulse begin to quicken. A dripping hairspray bottle, alcohol, water…think. I looked through my makeup kit and quickly grabbed the airbrush. I dumped out the foundation and rinsed the airbrush reservoir clean. I managed to pour some hairspray into the airbrush, adding a bit of rubbing alcohol and water to dilute, and prayed. I gave it a quick stir and tested it in the air. Voila! Airbrush hairspray. I quickly finished up Dan's hair; the show must go on.

As I begin to relax a bit and take in the excitement of the launch, I am approached by our producer. Someone from another network needed help. "Hair and makeup is not here; can you step in and help out, touch up a guest?" As a courtesy, the CBS producer asked me if this was okay, and off I went.

I quickly packed up a few cosmetics and moved to another staging area. How does this happen? Set up, apply, tear down, set up, apply, tear down again. Whew! I smile to myself, feeling as though I'm reading the directions on a bottle of shampoo.

I often, to this day, find myself wanting to retract something coming out of my mouth almost as simultaneously as I'm saying it. Perhaps it's my dry, deadpan sense of wit. Perhaps it's my being raised with four brothers. Perhaps it's my lack of formal education. Once we were on the hurry-up-and-wait train, I'm sitting and talking with Dan and say that I wanted to be sure to stop by the gift shop at Cape Canaveral, to pick up a souvenir for my daughter. I casually mention that I want to get a "blow-up astronaut," a child-sized superhero meant to inspire, especially girls. As I'm saying it, I see a pained expression come over his face. I'm wishing desperately that I could reel my statement back in. Having been on four different NASA stories now, following the tragic explosion of the Challenger, he says to me, "You might want to use a different choice of words." *Inflatable...inflatable astronaut.*

As the launch nears, the excitement in the room is palpable. I so wanted to leave the room with the viewing window, to run outside and see the launch from full view, not obstructed by the window. I'm remembering the exhilaration of the Discovery launch in 1988. Would it have the same effect on me? Certainly not. It's like seeing the Grand Canyon for the first time. Nothing could be so grand.

I was wrong. The concentration. The calm voice. The focal point. The rumble. The countdown. "FIVE. FOUR. THREE. TWO. ONE. ZERO. AND LIFTOFF." The elation. I watch John

Glenn and these brave and selfless astronauts travel into space, and again I'm crying happy tears.

Lyndon B. Johnson Space Center - Houston, Texas

NASA Shuttle Launch

LuAnn Mancini - 1960s

"Young Entrepreneur"

We sat in the front seat of her 1964 Ford Galaxy. The automobile was a powder blue, which matched her eyes. The car was in pristine condition, always kept immaculately clean, like her home on Egbert Street. Purchasing a used vehicle was out of the question. The car was parked in the small, detached garage for safekeeping. It must not be parked on the street in the elements of the harsh winters and should only be treated with the utmost of care.

The local mechanic would service the car regularly, whether it needed it or not. It was a low mileage vehicle, only being driven for errands within the small community of Brighton and the two-block drive to church on Sundays. On special occasions, she would drive twenty-three miles to visit the Archdiocese of Denver.

My grandmother looked out over the top of the steering wheel, and I was on the passenger side, sitting on the bench seat looking up at her as she spoke. At that time, children would ride in the front seat, unrestrained by a seat belt. I was just a young girl, the fourth child born to the expanding family of her youngest son and the first female following a set of three older brothers. My mother was overjoyed to be able to dress me in ruffles and lace after the long, drawn-out period of denim and plaid.

We sat in the parking lot of the bank, waiting for it to open. She looked directly at me when she spoke.

"You need to have a good doctor, someone who knows you. And more importantly, you need to have a good banker that you have your whole life. They need to know your face and your voice. Don't go through the drive-through."

She impressed upon me that it was important to be savvy in business. Looking back as an adult woman, for a woman in the 1960s to be self-sufficient was, in itself, remarkable. I didn't grow up playing dress up or playing house. I grew up wanting to be creative and innovative.

I have no memory of my grandfather. He passed away the year I was born. My grandma was a shrewd businesswoman, and many would say that she wore the pants in the family. The story is told that, coming from a farming background, she would let the green beans rot on the truck before accepting a low-ball offer from the owners of the vegetable market stand.

And thus began the entrepreneurial spirit of my heritage. Create enterprise. Money meant freedom. If I sold lemonade at my makeshift lemonade stand, I had the freedom to buy myself a candy bar. If I then bought candy for one dollar, I sold it for two dollars. Halloween meant the opportunity to create a haunted house in our dusty garage for the neighborhood children and, more importantly, to charge admission.

One hot summer day, we spent the afternoon creating a restaurant in our backyard. My mother was at work, employed in the costume jewelry department at the local mall. We were left to entertain ourselves. My sisters and I dusted off the picnic table, scavenged through the refrigerator to see what we could sell, created handwritten menus, and then started advertising to the children in the neighborhood that the restaurant was open for business. Hot dogs, chips, and candy for twenty-five cents. Peanut butter and jelly for ten cents.

My mother returned home from work later that evening, exhausted and ready to take off her confining clothing. She held in her hand her tired and worn shoe bag containing her pump heels, which she wore when working. We surrounded her as she came through the door with news of our venture. To her dismay, we proudly announced how much money we had made selling hot dogs, chips, and sandwiches for cents on the dollar. I recall the wide-eyed wonder from my mother, somewhat in disbelief. She explained to us that we were selling our groceries for far less than what we had paid for them with food stamps and that we should not do it any longer. I can still hear the defeat in her voice, emotionally drained by the few prospects in the refrigerator for the dinner meal.

I guess my grandmother was saving the profit and loss lesson for later.

Moscow Summit
May 29 - June 3, 1989

"Trial by Fire"

As I began my preparations, I thought, *I've never been out of the country before. This will be fun.* To say that I was very naive about foreign travel was an understatement. CBS had phoned to ask if I could leave town for two weeks to travel to the Soviet Union. Apparently, the impression I left on CBS was favorable, and I was asked to be part of the team travelling to Russia for the Moscow Summit between President Ronald Reagan and Mikhail Gorbachev.

We would first travel to New York, then on to Moscow the following day. The news was live from New York, and I would have the chance to meet one of the morning co-anchors that would be travelling to the USSR as part of the team. *Perfect,* I thought. I did my homework, watched several episodes of the morning news to study the face and the makeup, and made sure I had the right color palette. *I know exactly what I'm going to do to improve her current makeup, and she will love me, like all of the women I have worked on.*

What I didn't know at the time is what I was stepping into, the back story. Apparently, this person had a well-earned reputation.

Once in New York, I entered the small lobby of the network and was greeted by the receptionist. I introduced myself as a makeup artist for Dan Rather. After only a short wait, I was escorted through the hallways of the network to the control room. I was in awe of everything around me, everywhere I looked. Television anchors dating back to the beginning of CBS were in large, framed photos, arranged chronologically down the hallway. The control room was the size of my living room, with floor-to-ceiling panels of equipment and dials, screens, headsets, and microphones. *I've made it,* I thought to myself. *My clients will be so impressed.*

I watched as the live broadcast continued. It felt very prestigious, being able to observe first-hand. I was anxious to prove myself. It was always harder to break the ice with women, more so than men. I've often felt that women feel more comfortable with men, and men are more often at ease with a woman makeup artist or hair stylist.

I was politely told to wait…and wait…and wait. I observed the comings and goings of the people passing through, almost as if I were waiting for the next bus. I checked my watch, watching the minutes tick away. Every minute spent in the control room was one less minute I would have to meet with her.

After what seemed like an eternity, at some point I was informed that she had already gone home for the day. We never had the chance to meet. I chalked it off to a miscommunication, that she truly didn't have time to meet with me. I'm the new kid on the block. I was paid well to be there. It's not a problem. I will have many opportunities in the upcoming days to come, "across the pond." I made my way back to the hotel and prepared for the international flight the following day.

The World Trade Center attack in September 2001 was well in front of us. The airlines were still allowing me to have my makeup kit on board. I could not risk being separated from my "art supplies." I think back now to the strict restrictions put in place by the airlines and wonder how I would get my creams, foundation, and "hazardous materials" on the plane if I were making the same trip today. I'm glad those days are behind me.

I boarded the Aeroflot plane, full of excitement, anticipating what Russia would be like. I need look no further. From the moment I stepped onto the plane, I already felt like I was in the USSR, immediately thrust into another culture. Dim lighting and dirty bathrooms greeted me onto the flight. It was a very large plane, and

I was funneled with the crowds of people into the back of the cabin, seated on an elevated portion with shallow head clearance. The accents were heavy, the processed microwaved food was flat and flavorless, and the plane was not what I would call first-class travel.

If that wasn't a wake-up call, to add insult to injury, the man seated beside me wanted to become better acquainted. He was a New York/Jersey kind of looking gentleman, a bit cocky. At first flirting and playful, he then decided to hit on me and wanted to neck and make out. The male dominated world of broadcasting was evident in the late '80s, and business travel was no different. I made it clear to him that his advances were not welcome.

After a long and arduous flight, we landed safely in Moscow, and I was ready to begin the adventure. As the sun began to rise and peeked over the horizon, the hotel shuttle van pulled up to greet us, efficiently equipped with luggage tags, security papers, and press passes. Everything we needed to be escorted through the gates of security in Moscow was at our disposal.

The team made our way to Hotel Rossiya, located squarely in the center of the city in Red Square. After a twenty-two-hour flight, we had finally arrived. Our van pulled into the circle drive, and I was taken aback at the worn and tired building. "In its day" the hotel was undoubtedly a showpiece, a statement of grand proportions, but those days were long gone.

Charles Kuralt and Maria Shriver greeted each other in the parking lot, respected colleagues in their field. *I have arrived,* I thought to myself. The beautiful display of St. Basil's Cathedral could be seen in the distance, just a short walk from the hotel. Again, being quite naive, I thought, *Hmmm. Looks like Disneyland.*

Although I was honored to have been asked by CBS to travel, it was, after all, still the Soviet Union. The exterior of the hotel was a wall of more than 3,000 hotel rooms lacking any architectural design and personality, with row after row of windows resembling a hospital or compound. We were fortunate to have all of our workspaces located together in the hotel, but our personal hotel rooms were spread out in the hotel over many floors.

When I entered my hotel room, the accommodations resembled what you might find in a $65 hotel room in New York—a two-inch mattress on the bed frame and drab colored upholstery. I saw yet more glass resembling the exterior of the building, seeing my reflection in every direction I looked. Walls and walls of mirrors. It brought me back to the walls of a fun house at an amusement park, never knowing which wall was a mirror and which wall would open as a secret passageway. Perhaps I've watched too many *Get Smart* television episodes as a child, with Maxwell Smart and Agent 99, but I had the strangest feeling that I was being watched, even when I was alone.

By this time, I was very sleep deprived and a bit giddy, and I uneasily tried to settle into my hotel room. I walked closer to the mirrors, leaned in close, and started talking to them. At this point I began laughing, thinking about the mythological KGB spies watching me from the basement of the hotel.

"Okay," I said out loud. "If you're going to watch me, I'm going to give you something to look at."

I started to dance, alone in my hotel room, pulling off pieces of clothing one at a time like a strip tease, shielding myself with my bath towel. It had been a very long day of travel. I could only envision my imagined spies in the basement saying, "Hey, Dmitri! Come over here, you gotta see this," in Russian, of course. I have always been accused of being a bit quirky. Was it my overactive imagination, or were the Russian men smiling at me on the set in the following days to come, my imagined spies from the basement of the Rossiya Hotel? By the end of the week, I concluded that mirrors or not, being watched or not, I had more important things to think about.

Our workspaces were assigned, and thankfully we were all on the same floor of the hotel. What seemed odd, however, is that I was designated to share workspace with David, the Vice President of

News. Perhaps I was just the odd person needing a home. It meant running the entire length of the hotel, back and forth to get supplies, then back to the set. Again, I'm the newbie. I can make this work.

Security was high while on this trip, which probably didn't help my paranoia. Whenever I left my work room, whether it be to stretch my legs or to grab a cup of coffee, upon my return they would "wand" both the room and my person. Because we were working with high profile government figures, both Russian and American, upon my return I would watch as they "swept" the room for explosives, microphones, and cameras. Once the room was cleared and signed off, I was allowed to re-enter. After a few episodes of this time-consuming procedure, I recognized it would probably be best if I sat my hyper-self down in the room and waited for my next job assignment.

I'm not often afforded a lot of time to work. Most times I'm applying makeup while someone is being mic'd up, reading a script, or preparing notes. I'm invisible. The good news is that because most of the broadcasters at that time were men, it required only a few items: powder, sponges, contour, hairspray, and a comb. In the1990s, fanny packs were especially in vogue, and I would carry what I needed on my person. Tissues filled my pocket, and a lint roller was shoved in my back pocket; I was "packing." There was no place to physically set up a workstation on the set.

The time had come to meet her, the morning co-host. Now I could introduce myself properly and hopefully "wow" her—a blank palette waiting for my artistry. I couldn't wait! I stood like an excited school child on their first day of kindergarten on the steps of the school. I introduced myself to her hair stylist, learning that we had a total of twenty minutes to do both hair and makeup on our co-anchor. I suggested that perhaps we could split the difference and each have ten minutes, rather than trying to apply eye liner, shadow, and lipstick to a moving target when she was having her hair blown out and styled. We came to an agreement that this could work.

As she walked into the room, I extended my arms and handed her my portfolio, almost like an open Bible, exposing all of my truths. Displayed was all of my most prestigious work, with professional makeup that she would easily recognize.

"I'm so excited to meet you," I said. "I've watched you on the morning news. I've brought some examples of my work."

She briskly snaps it closed with a determined expression and replies somewhat indignantly, "I'm in television. That's print." She then turns to look at my workspace and says, "I'll be doing my own makeup. Your products are not professional."

Okay…welcome aboard.

Products have changed over the years, but "back in the day," in 1988, 99 percent of makeup artists purchased their products from the same wholesale supplier. Because I had been in business for myself for over ten years, had my own studio, and had specifically created and packaged my own private label, my products were probably not recognizable to her. She just didn't know it.

Trial by fire, "a test of one's abilities to perform well under pressure." My first big job, the first day on a two-week gig…it rattled me.

I made the decision to take care of everyone else, but I privately wondered how long it was going to take CBS to notice that she wasn't in professional makeup. *Is New York going to notice?*

It didn't take but a day for me to get that answer. They reached out to Dan's people. While doing his makeup, he asked me privately, "What is going on with her makeup? New York is not happy. Aren't you doing her makeup?"

"No," I replied confidentially. "She won't let me touch her."

CBS had never seen me do a woman's makeup. I could have been that bad. They trusted me, having seen Dan's makeup. Makeup on a male, mind you. Perhaps they were trusting recommendations or referrals. But I specialized in women. That was my forte. That was my specialty. My ego was bruised, but worse, it triggered my temper. I wanted to turn this situation around. I was on her side. If she didn't like what I did, I would change it. Trial by fire.

In a studio setting with a union looking over your shoulder, there would be a makeup artist for the morning news and another makeup artist for the evening news. Because we were on location and were limited to how many people could travel, there would be only one makeup artist. As it turns out, as I came to later learn, Dan got to select the makeup artist, and she got to select the hair stylist. She was pissed.

As I would touch up the makeup for the guests, it was always a moving target. Step in, cape them, quick makeup in two minutes, uncape, and move back out. No time for introductions, just get it done. At this point, she didn't even know my name. What was a tense situation from the start continued to deteriorate. When I would make up a man, she would comment, "Look at all this makeup. This is too much makeup for a man."

I tried to stay out of the line of fire. When we were "on the air," I would move to the back of the room because I realized there was friction. In between guests, I would hide between rows of technicians, a safe retreat. At one point when we were on the air, the executive producer dropped his headset from his hand, and it hit the floor with a loud crash. I was standing directly behind him, yet leaning against the wall with my arms crossed. As soon as we went to commercial, she turns and points her finger directly at me, a very deliberate gesture.

What's the beef? I thought. Everybody turns and looks.

"I don't want you in here when I'm on the set."

Caught off guard and totally humiliated, I left the set and went down what seemed like an endless hallway, all the while trying not to cry. I was pissed. Being from an emotional Italian family, when I'm angry, the result is waterworks. It's just the way it works. By this time, I cannot control my anger, and I am in tears. I went into my workspace, the makeup room, and there I am, now with the VP of news. He was a hardy New Yorker, a people person who had nothing to prove. He had been around the block a few times, a down to earth kind of guy.

"What's the matter? What's wrong?" he says.

"I don't go halfway around the world to be treated like shit!"

"Who's treating you like shit?" he responded accordingly.

"She, who shall remain nameless," I respond.

"Oh, don't worry about it. She treats everybody like shit." Trial by fire.

Let the games begin. Once word got out, the crew started sharing stories with me. According to them, on any one trip she would single out one person and pick on that person. Apparently, I had won the lottery.

At one point, about two or three days in, I found myself working in the hallway to do makeup, to try and stay out of the way. My kit is strung out in the hallway, on the floor and along the walls. Dan comes along and quizzically asks, "What are you doing in the hallway? What is going on?"

"I'm not allowed on the set."

"Why not?"

"She doesn't want me on the set while she's on air."

He gave me the look, *You've got to be kidding.*

He opens the door and gestures, "Makeup needs to be on the set. You're not working in the hallway." He refused to allow me to work in the hallway and on the floor.

There was a silent struggle going on between the two journalists. Every time there was a commercial, Dan would call out, "Makeup! I need some powder." What was most humorous about this encounter was that he didn't even like powder. He wasn't going to let the shenanigans go on. Point made. *What have I got myself in the middle of?* What I regret most about this scenario is that I never got to do her makeup.

Once we were underway, I had bigger fish to fry. I was focused on the tasks at hand. Travelling with a network as prestigious as CBS, my path crossed with greatness many times over. While on the trip, I did Andrew Lloyd Webber's makeup. Gorbachev was a fan of *Cats,* and they were there to perform for him during the summit. Again,

I was taken aback that a man who was this brilliant was so humble. If you didn't know it was Andrew Lloyd Webber, he would seem to be just another man on the street. I think I inaccurately assumed that he would be a showman, such as Liberace. Then again, he was a composer, not a performer. He left the drama to the actors. I regret not having more time to ask him some questions. I was intrigued by the extravagant makeup of *Cats* and wanted to know more.

While on this trip, I also had the opportunity to do makeup for both the late Secretary George Schultz and the late General Colin Powell, whom I refer to as "the gentle giant." They were both travelling with their wives. Again, I was struck by the quiet confidence of greatness that they exhibited, the weight of the world on their shoulders. Their stoic reserve immediately set me at ease, knowing that our country was in their hands. The greater the man, the humbler the persona.

I remember receiving one of the nicest compliments I have ever received while doing makeup for Secretary Schultz. I offered him a mirror for him to see if he approved of my work.

"Do you need a mirror? Do you want to see how it looks?"

"No, I can see that I'm in the hands of a professional." It was always such a welcome change to work on men. I did not have to first earn their confidence.

I also had the opportunity to work on Russian dignitaries, under the discerning lens, or I should say lack thereof, of Vladimir Putin. All were on guard, and you could sense their uneasiness and tension in the air.

What I distinctly recall is that I could not get Vladimir Putin to make eye contact. It was such an unusual encounter and a cold feeling, when working so close in proximity to someone. I think Joe Biden said it best, in an article by *The Hill*. "As I turned, I was this close to him," Biden said, signaling that the two leaders were standing just inches apart. "I said, 'Mr. Prime Minister, I'm looking into your eyes, and I don't think you have a soul.'"

The most memorable event that occurred during the Moscow trip was an event that was held at the Moscow Operetta Theatre. It was to take place at roughly 9:00 p.m. local time, to coordinate with the Eastern Time Zone back in New York. I arrived promptly in the lobby of the Rossiya Hotel, anxiously looking for my group. No one was anywhere to be seen. I waited for a short bit and quickly realized something was amiss. Somehow, amidst the chaos of the itinerary, I had been left behind. I was panicked. I knew it was a live broadcast, and there would be no time for error. If I wasn't there, they would go on air without makeup. *There goes my career with CBS.*

I quickly gathered my thoughts, but also my belongings. I fortunately had some Russian rubles and dashed out to the circle drive. There were a few cars out front—square, boxy caricatures of a taxicab with hard, black leather upholstery. It was a beautiful summer night, and I distinctly remember looking up and seeing a full moon. I stepped into the back seat of the cab and asked the cabby if he spoke English. He replied, no. Here I was, in a foreign socialist country, no one knew where I was or where I was going, getting into a cab with a man that didn't speak English. I asked myself, *Is this where my life ends? Am I going to end up in a ditch somewhere? Is he taking me to the Moscow Operetta Theatre or the Bolshoi Opera House? Where will I end up?*

I didn't have a cell phone at that time. I had to trust fate, and it was a risk I had to take.

The cabby pulled away from the curb, and I summoned him to pull over and stop. I didn't know where he thought he was going. The only means of communication I had was to try a spirited game of Charades. I first tried "makeup, lights, camera, big, beautiful chandelier." From the blank expression on his face, I could see I was having no luck. Then I decided to go big, full arm gestures, singing in a loud voice, attempting to imitate an opera singer. For anyone that knows me, the musical talent in the family did not go to me.

He nodded affirmatively at me and then pulled the automobile away from the curb. Racing through the Moscow traffic, within a few short minutes we pulled up to the Moscow Operetta Theatre, where I could see the CBS truck parked and already unloaded. I then realized that there was no meter in the cab, nor did I speak Russian. I pulled out my Russian rubles, my Monopoly money, and held the bills and coins in the palms of my two hands for him to take what he needed for the cab ride. I do not to this day know how much he took, nor if I was being taken advantage of. It was the least of my worries in that moment.

I raced inside, sweaty and in a bit of a frenzy. The four journalists were already mic'd up, on stage, and in position to broadcast a round table panel. As I try to scurry onto the stage, I am reprimanded by the ushers for having my rolling kit on the carpet of the opera house, and I had to carry it onto the stage. In a flurry of scolding the four men for leaving me, I quickly applied their makeup, making up for lost time. Somehow, I had managed to dodge that bullet, once again, although a little too close for comfort. I think I'll hold off on my audition for the Bolshoi Opera. Trial by fire.

St. Basil's Cathedral. "It looks like Disneyland!"

GUM Department Store – Ushanka hat!

Round Table Panel – Moscow Operetta Theatre

Czech Republic, Russia, Prague, Moscow - January 1994

"The Tale of Two Moscows"

The more I travelled, the less I knew. I found myself in awe of the world before me, the world I did not know. I walked the streets of the Czech Republic, hearing the sounds of the Moody Blues playing over the loudspeakers, feeling the forward thinking of this small country becoming Americanized. I was travelling in the lap of luxury, able to purchase extravagances for a fraction of the price on the U.S. dollar.

After our planned week in Moscow in 1988, our trip concluded with a scurried thirty-minute trip to GUM department store, one of many beautiful displays of architecture in the city. The American influence had begun to reach Moscow. I saw stores that I recognized, such as Estee Lauder and Levi's. My translator, Mila, was a local Russian woman who helped me navigate the language. Most of my colleagues were purchasing the traditional Stolichnaya Vodka, but despite my Italian heritage, I'm not much of a drinker. I decided on a traditional black ushanka, a Russian men's hat trimmed in fur, and a sturdy pair of Russian boots, thinking that this was the wiser purchase to transport home in a suitcase.

In June of 1988, I boarded the Aeroflot plane to return to the USA. Fast forward, and in January of 1994, I walked back off the

plane in Moscow, wearing the same ushanka hat that I had purchased in 1988 at the GUM department store. The trip six years
prior was a beautiful time of year, graced with mild weather. Now,
amidst winter, it gave me the opportunity to wear my souvenir,
which I never thought I would have the chance to do in the heat of
Texas. The frozen snow, muddy puddles, and ice were tell-tale signs
of the harsh winter weather of the northern hemisphere.

President Bill Clinton was meeting with President Boris Yeltsin
to sign a nuclear disarmament agreement with Ukraine, and CBS
would again travel to Moscow to cover the story.

I stepped onto the airport shuttle to find that I was one of only
two passengers on the bus; the other was Dan Rather. We greeted
each other like family, getting together once again for the annual
family reunion. There were no seats on the shuttle. I held on tightly
to the overhead vinyl strap as we bumped along the tracks on our
way to the terminal, while trying to manage both of my two makeup
kits. As we engaged in casual conversation, he looked at the hat on
my head, oversized and obviously from the men's department, and
chuckled.

"Where did you get that?"

I laughed and said that I had purchased it on our last trip to
Moscow, in 1988. He chuckled in response, obviously amused. Dan
is what I might call an intense person, always striving to get the
story, with truth and integrity, and he didn't loosen up very often.
It was always nice to see him laugh.

After the long flight, followed by going through customs and
the shuttle ride, it was gratifying to finally be arriving at the hotel.
The city looked noticeably different this time. The streets were
filled with people, the hustle and bustle. I noticed that the absence
of color from 1988, the dull and drab gray that encapsulated the
city, was no longer—it was now more colorful. We stepped into the
lobby, and I was immediately taken aback. The hotel had become
Americanized, the best that money could buy, with capitalism being

fully embraced by the Russian culture. It was clearly different than just six years earlier.

The workspaces of the network were being set up off the main lobby of the hotel for easy access, and crate after crate of equipment was already unloaded by the technicians and ready to go. After checking in at the front desk, and with the help of a valet, I found my way to my room to be further pleasantly surprised by the extravagance. The down duvet was thicker than thick, and the towels were heated to perfection. I walked through the room to set down my toiletries in the bathroom, observing marble on the vanity and in every direction I looked. Feeling very worldly and deserving of a blue ribbon, I was able to recognize the bidet in my lavatory, now fully realizing it was not, in fact, two his and hers porcelain toilets.

I also learned that there was a heated swimming pool in the basement of the hotel, which would be a wonderful reprieve if I was ever able to break away for a small bit of time for myself.

On one of the days to follow, CBS was going to do a piece about the black market in Moscow. Coincidentally, I was able to witness small pockets of police corruption. If you wanted a parking spot on the street, you had two options: offer them a pack or two of cigarettes or be towed. It was an arrangement that was well understood.

I went to Dan Rather's room to prepare his makeup for the day so that he could be on his way and out onto the streets. With the harsh winter underway, he would clearly be out of place in a suit, and he pieced together an outfit with a pair of jeans, boots, a canvas jacket, and a large overcoat. As if by déjà vu, I proposed an idea. I offered him my Russian ushanka hat to wear.

"It's a man's hat. Do you want to borrow it? Take it with you and maybe you can use it in a few pieces." I quickly retrieved the fur symbol of Russian residency and brought it back to his room. Dan was a man of authenticity. If the hat were not made in Russia, or if it were a woman's hat, he would not be seen wearing it. As it turns out, my hat showed up in a few CBS stories, a welcome retreat from the bitter cold.

My business trips with CBS were very unpredictable. I never knew whether I would be needed first thing in the morning, many times during the day, or for only the evening news. After sending him on his way, I checked in with headquarters to confirm the rest of my day.

"No, no. He'll be out for two to three hours. You're released. Would you like to get some sleep? Check back in two hours."

With the dreary weather outside, I was chilled to the bone, and I felt like it would be a nice respite to visit the heated pool in the basement of the hotel for a long-needed bit of exercise.

This is where the story starts to sound like a B-rate James Bond movie. The pool was a wonderful oasis, away from the hurried tourists in the lobby. I had the pool to myself, enjoying the languid moment. The water was a tepid temperature. The lighting was dim, a tranquil mood falling over the large room. I was in the water for no longer than ten minutes and began doing my laps when an associate came rushing into the pool area to summon my attention. He was moving with such urgency that I thought perhaps there was an emergency. *Is there a fire? Is there a terrorist threat?*

He is yelling at me, "We got the interview!"

I hadn't known that this interview was in the works, but CBS had secured an interview with Bill Clinton, and we needed to go right away. Right now. Immediately.

Because I worked in a male dominated profession, I always tried to dress professionally, but never with any sexual connotations. No cleavage, no high heels, minimal jewelry, no heavy makeup. In a quick but awkward thirty seconds, we are looking at each other like Elliot and ET from the 1982 film—two strange beings wondering who each other is or what each other wants.

I was standing on the pool deck in my wet swimsuit, hair dripping down my shoulders. He was startled and said somewhat awkwardly, "I don't know how to recognize you without your clothes." I reached for a bath towel to wrap myself with and gather my belongings.

I'm not even dried off, yet I'm running down the hallway, leaving a trail of footprints on the carpet. There was no time for a shower, and I probably wreaked of chlorine. I was out of the door, huffing and puffing, within moments of pulling my clothes on. My hair was not even dry, but I was sweating, nonetheless, because I am stressed. I grab my makeup kit, and I'm headed to the lobby to meet with the team.

As I made my way through the crew, I found our producer, Wayne. We began to discuss the logistics of the interview, when I realized that the interview was not going to take place at our hotel, but the hotel where President Clinton and the press corps were staying. I was happy to oblige, but quickly reminded Wayne that Dan had left the hotel this morning in jeans and boots. It would hardly be the attire he would want to be dressed in to interview the President of the United States.

"He doesn't have his suit?" Wayne asked.

"Remember? He went out on a story!" I replied.

"We've got to find Dan, and we've got to get Dan's suit!"

The producer was caught off guard, but we quickly decided that they would round up Dan, and I would gather his clothes from his hotel room and take them to the site of the interview. Or so I thought that was the understanding.

At this point the story becomes more Keystone Cops on steroids, less James Bond and his smooth sophistication. I quickly ran to the front desk, lacking any knowledge of the Russian language, and explained to the personnel that I needed a key to Dan Rather's room, to get his clothes for the interview with Bill Clinton, the U.S. President. I was wearing my CBS credentials on a lanyard around my neck. I rattled through my explanation, and I must have been very persuasive, because within five minutes I was in the room, gathering his articles of clothing.

"I'm going to leave my makeup kit at the front door," I said to the front desk. "I'm going to need a cab. Could you tell the cabby where I need to go," said more as a command than a question.

Somehow in the heat of the moment, I had thought ahead. I did not want to relive the Moscow Operetta Theatre Charades pantomime with the cab driver. I headed for the elevator and ran up to his room.

Once in his room, I expected to find a suit and tie and perhaps a pair of shoes. There were two suits, two pairs of shoes, and many shirts and ties, all monogrammed with his signature hurricane on the sleeve. In September of 1961, Dan Rather covered Hurricane Carla in Galveston, Texas and had "a damn fool idea" to strap himself to a tree to avoid being swept away. It was because of that coverage that he got his "First Big Break" with CBS.

What would he like to wear? What would he prefer to wear to interview the President of the United States?

Rather than debate with myself, I grabbed it all. A couple of suits, many pressed, starched shirts, ties, and shoes. I threw the clothing over my arm and shoved the shoes into a satchel.

At this point, I was still unclear about how much time we had, but my worst nightmare would have been that President Clinton would be kept waiting or that Dan would not be fully prepped before the President's arrival.

Within twenty minutes of getting rounded up from the pool, I was hailing a cab. Had I truly known how long we had, I would have thought this through a little more carefully. As I'm stepping over gray puddles of slush and snow to get into the cab, I questioned my decision to grab the clothes without first putting them into a garment bag.

I reach up to wipe my furrowed brow and pull the hair from my face and realize that it is crispy, still wet from the swimming pool and frozen from the frigid temperatures. The two hotels were fairly close in proximity, and feeling as though time were slipping away, I sighed in relief as we pulled up to the Slavyanskaya Radisson Hotel—clothing, two makeup kits, and a satchel with two pairs of dress shoes in tow.

I fully anticipated walking onto the set with everyone in place. To my great relief, I was one of the first to arrive. The crew was busily setting up the set. I laid out his clothes and tried to gather myself. I fluffed my hair to let it dry. I wiped the black smudges of mascara out from under my eyes.

Then we wait, and wait, and wait. Forty-five minutes later, I begin to worry that something has gone very wrong. Finally, Wayne, the senior producer, scurries in, looking rather harried. Forcefully and rather firmly he says to me, "Where are Dan's suits?"

"You told me to get them. I got Dan's clothes!"

"He's back at the hotel, looking for his suits." *There goes my career. The emperor has no clothes.* Trial by fire.

When Dan got upset, which was not very often, he was usually very forgiving. But if somebody was not carrying their weight or messing up, you didn't usually see them again on the set. They didn't get fired; they just didn't get to work with him. After he had calmed down, he was very forgiving, and it could usually be worked out.

Wayne grabs the clothes, as the crew is standing by and watching this unfold. You could read the expressions on their faces. They know there's something going on. Whenever something would start to go awry, the set would get quiet and everyone would scatter, suddenly in need of a cup of coffee or wanting to return an urgent phone call.

Once the situation was now out of my control, it was time to wait, and wait, and wait. Again. It was probably another forty-five minutes of painstaking waiting to see who would arrive first, Dan Rather or President Clinton. If Bill Clinton were to arrive before Dan Rather, my ass is grass. I would have been toast. Dan would have been so upset. Then, after an abominably long wait, he comes walking in, in his suit.

In a frenzy of nervous energy, I began to explain.

"We'll talk about it later," he said shortly. I could only envision the steam coming out of his ears.

"Okay," I said quietly. I had to get his makeup on him as fast as I could. And within the blink of an eye, within ten minutes Bill

Clinton walks in. Everyone on guard, on their best behavior, they all stand to formally greet the 42nd President.

Then, according to protocol, and as if the last two hours had been a mirage, "LuAnn is here to touch up your makeup, Mr. President, if you'd like."

"Yes, that would be fine."

He glanced at me, the wheels turning as to why I looked familiar to him. I shifted my makeup cape to the other arm and held out my hand to greet him.

Applying makeup to a male, in my mind, is fairly straightforward. It requires no eyeshadow, eyeliner, lipstick, blush, eyelash curlers, and on and on. Everything I use can be on my person. In many cases I don't even have a kit, just my fanny pack, my trusted "holster."

For security reasons, the Secret Service had to first check my makeup kit. Then, as if on automatic pilot, I swoop in, cape him, then tape and cuff him so as not to get makeup on his clothes. If someone is wearing glasses, I remove them. If they are not wearing glasses, I will inquire if they are wearing contact lenses.

At this point in the chaos, I was the one slowing down the show. My typical ten to twelve minutes per face is now cut to four or five minutes. I'm pulling tissues from one pocket, the lint brush out of my back pocket, like a gun from a holster, a cowboy in a spaghetti western. I'm moving very quickly to make up for lost time. Apparently, the Secret Service thought the same thing, as I see them flinch and react to my very quick movements, resembling a hyperactive poodle. I needed to slow down. Breathe.

President Clinton was an easy subject, a handsome man with a nice smile and a positive energy. I felt comfortable moving around him, because I had done his makeup previously, during his first run for office. I prepared Mr. Clinton's hair and face, retelling the story while trying to make him feel at ease. I also had the opportunity to do makeup for Hillary Clinton in 1993, while she was in D.C. preparing the health care package, and I shared that story with him, as well. Whether he was being a gracious politician or perhaps he had the memory of an elephant, he said that he had recognized me.

I hadn't checked either Dan or President Clinton on the monitor yet. The lighting is *always* different, which presents a challenge. By the time the guests are in place and on the set, we're usually sixty seconds out from the live broadcast. This is my last chance to use the lint brush or to hairspray a stray hair into place.

Doris Day sang a song in 1956 called "Que Sera, Sera." Loosely translated, "Whatever will be, will be." My job was finished. My stomach was in a knot, but it was out of my control.

When it was all said and done, we then took our "class picture." One picture, taken by the presidential photographer, Sharon Farmer. She would take names and later send an 8x10 photo. I wondered, and worried, whether she would follow through, with the hundreds of photos that must take place. To my joy she did, and an 8x10 horizontal photo arrived at my studio. I was standing smack in the middle, the only female in the group. Dan Rather was standing on my left, and President Clinton was standing on my right. And to my revelation, my makeup and hair looked pretty good for being beckoned from the swimming pool.

When the tension of the interview was over and the adrenaline was gone, at that point I just wanted to know one thing. I finally had the courage to approach Dan and initiate a conversation.

"What?" Dan asked.

"Did I do the right thing by going to get your clothes?"

"You did the right thing. We don't have to talk about it."

"I didn't know if I missed the cue from Wayne. I saw how you left the hotel."

"We got the job done."

As I think back on this trip, I have many thoughts. One of them probably wouldn't be that I had "dodged a bullet." More accurately stated was that I was wearing a bulletproof vest, being pelted repeatedly. It was a scene that I wish never to repeat. Trial by fire.

An interview concluded our final days while in Moscow, with Harry Smith as the moderator, one of CBS's morning hosts for over seventeen years. While it was commonplace for me to do the makeup for any guests, the Russian dignitary was accompanied by his own makeup artist. The female makeup artist was also a Russian born citizen and was fairly comfortable with the English language. She was a pretty, young woman in her early thirties, with a warm smile and blonde hair. She fit the description of someone who worked with makeup. We both enjoyed the glamour, two professionals in the industry.

We were cordial with each other and worked side by side to achieve a common goal. I did not feel any artistic friction. I looked on at her supplies, saddened by the meager tools she was working with. Her cosmetics were limited, and her brushes were old and had a limp, sparse amount of hair remaining in them. It bothered me that I had so much and that she had so little. I think at that point I gave her a concealer or a contour powder.

She returned the following day with a hand painted plate, a hobby that she and her mother shared. It was a very primitive piece of art, but the gesture was so grand it touched me; she was wanting to return the kindness for my gift of makeup. We parted with a heart-felt hug, never to meet again.

My colleagues were always looking out for me and each other, our CBS family, and I, likewise, wanted to pay it forward. When I spoke with CBS New York, they confirmed that they send shipments periodically to their team in Moscow and assured me that they could forward a package to my newest makeup colleague in Russia.

Back in Fort Worth, Texas, I began to assemble a care package with a few supplies to send to her, and it quickly ballooned into a very generous gift of several hundred dollars. The inequities of our supplies were troubling, mine and hers, and I knew, having watched her work, that given the right tools, she would know how to use them correctly. I can only imagine that when she received the package it felt like Christmas. Truth be known, sending the gift of cosmetics brought me as much joy as she likely gained from receiving it.

Hurricane Carla - September 1961

KHOU archival video https://danratherjournalist.org/ground/natural-disasters/hurricane-carla/video-hurricane-carla-rather-report

My First Big Break

https://danratherjournalist.org/ground/natural-disasters/hurricane-carla/video-rather-remembers-hurricane-carla

LuAnn Mancini - 1975

"Forks in the Road"

I looked out over an ocean of blue. I sat in the hard steel folding chairs amidst the broad expanse of grass on the football field, trying not to fidget. In the direct Colorado sun, I could feel the fabric stuck to the back of my legs. We were at the Jeffco Stadium in Lakewood, Colorado, where graduations occur. The heat of the day was beating down, and I had not worn sunscreen. Certainly, someone would invent makeup with sunscreen in it, someday....

I was in a royal blue cap and gown, looking past the rows and rows of graduating high school seniors. Five hundred and eighty hopeful students with a plan. Many were college bound. Many had secured a job. In the '70s, a "gap year" was a foreign concept, literally and figuratively. Get on with life, secure your future, yet I had no plan.

I was not a good student. I was not even an average student. I felt as though there was nothing for me in high school. My senior year included a family planning class, office assistant to the principal's office, student government, and a financial planning class. Being female in the 1970s in a "financial planning" class meant being able to balance a checkbook. I was unable to pass the class, yet somehow, I scraped together enough credits to graduate from high school. Monday through Friday, I finished my minimal class load by noon and then went to work at the local mall.

And so began the search for "my passion." My high school had offered a career guidance class, and after a short course in 10 key, I tried my hand at secretarial work as a temp. I sat in the small, windowless reception room of an accountant. A dead plant sat limp in the corner. The door to the office remained open, ensuring that he could hear the machine churning as I methodically entered numbers. My boss was hoping for efficiency, as I entered the numbers into the device at the pace of a snail. It was one of the longest days of my life. I was not asked back, nor did I wish to return.

The valedictorian drug on and on. At times he was humorous, but mostly he used every cliche meant to inspire. We moved our white tassels from right to left. And finally, the painstaking process was over.

Following graduation from high school, I began working at the Denver Dry Goods Company. It was a high-end retail store, with pristine glass cases displaying the finest that money could buy. I worked in the makeup department, greeting and selling to patrons. I didn't know which direction my life was going to take me. What I did know is that I liked makeup, and I was a good salesman. I moved into an apartment, leaving behind me the security of a rent-free existence and many siblings, to now sharing square footage with two roommates and an open loft as a bedroom. I was also waiting tables at night. Because I did not own a car, I was taking public transit to work, catching a ride when I could, riding my bike when weather permitted, and if tips were good, I could afford a cab ride.

College was the traditional path, so I thought I would give it a whirl at the local community college on the Auraria campus. My means of transportation was to ride my bicycle in downtown traffic to get to my classes. When I met with a guidance counselor, she asked me, "What do you want to do?"

"I want to help people," I replied with confidence. And I meant it.

Without looking at my high school transcript and my grades, I was guided to consider a two-year degree in the medical field. I took the opportunity to tour the school for dental hygienists. I was not impressed. Or I should say, I was not favorably impressed.

I next considered becoming an ultrasound technician. I enrolled in medical terminology, along with medical anatomy, chemistry, and a basic English course for freshmen. I was overwhelmed and in over my head. I knew that I was totally unprepared for college and had no foundational knowledge in medicine. I sat in the classroom feeling as though I had walked into the wrong movie theater, with the actors speaking a foreign language, only there were no subtitles.

Even with all of this in mind, I thought that perhaps I might fail one course, but I could pull a rabbit out of a hat, and I would pass the other three. At the end of my first semester, I had failed all four courses. I could not retain the information. More importantly, I had no interest in this career path. I ended up dropping out of college after just one semester.

The thought of travel intrigued me, so I moved on to the travel industry. At nineteen years of age, I had never seen the ocean before, and I had never been on an airplane. Braniff Airlines was hiring stewardesses. "Come fly with me!" they touted. I had spent time waiting tables; how hard could it be? I boarded the airplane for the interview in the only business outfit I owned—my navy suit, pumps, and pantyhose. Hearing the seat belt buckle into place, I excitedly began to anticipate what an exciting lifestyle this could be. This is when I first reaffirmed that I had motion sickness concerns. More specifically, I vomited on my first airplane ride to an interview to work for the airlines. Riding roller coasters as a child was always challenging, but I had not put two and two together. This is not good.

As a young, impressionable girl, my high school years were not easy ones. Transitioning into the work force, it would have been very easy to go off the rails into a deep abyss. I look back at glimpses in time that were "a mine field," dodging what could have taken me down a very different and dark path.

When still in high school, I was intrigued by makeup, fashion, and beauty pageants, and I began working with a modeling agency. I never cared about being wealthy, but I wanted to become famous.

I wanted people to know my name. More importantly, I did not want to do without.

I began modeling assignments with the agency, dreaming of bigger things to come. The jobs were small ads, working at the local mall, once dressing the part of Santa's helper. Another job included "tearoom modeling," during happy hour, modeling clothing at a hotel near the airport, going from table to table and displaying outfits for sale. The event included modeling lingerie. Some of the sleepwear sold to patrons, but with wisdom that comes with age, I can only imagine that there were more things that were being sold than I was naively unaware of at the time.

A young model and I became friends. She was a beautiful girl, perhaps twenty-two or twenty-three years of age, with long hair the color of a sandy beach, highlighted in blonde. Not having been more than a Size 2, she was truly the girl next door. I looked up to her. She was spellbound by a young man whom she felt she loved, and she also believed that he was in love with her.

One snowy evening in Denver, the night of a dreary blizzard, she phoned me from her apartment.

"I worked all day. I don't have any food or money. He beat me up and took my clothes."

She had no clothing, she hadn't eaten that day, and her boyfriend took her car keys so that she could not leave the apartment. I didn't have many details, but I told my mother that I needed to help one of my friends and left that evening, in the snowstorm, on a mission of mercy.

I drove to her apartment that evening, stopping at Burger King to get food, and carried with me some jeans, a sweatshirt, tennis shoes, and a pair of socks from home. Walking into the dimly lit hallways of the complex, past the enclosed courtyard, I took the elevator up to the apartment, fearful of who I would confront on the other side of the doors and questioning whether this would be my last night on this Earth.

Her boyfriend never liked me. He wouldn't speak to me. I came to learn that he was not only what she believed to be her boyfriend, the man she felt she loved—he was also her pimp. A thug.

She didn't want to "work" anymore, and he beat her up. Looking back, it was like watching a horror movie. How it must feel to be trapped, held prisoner by someone you loved, was beyond my understanding. I worried that he might be waiting and stalking her, or me, in the parking lot.

She opened the door, barefoot and wrapped in a sheet, with disheveled hair and a bruised face. After striking her, he told her that if she wouldn't work for him, that he would ensure that she could no longer model for anyone else.

I looked into her, now, bloody and swollen eyes, trying to read her thoughts. She was clearly overwhelmed and couldn't see past one day at a time, with no foresight for what the future might hold. An expression of relief washed across her face, like a caged animal trapped and fighting for survival.

Stepping into the apartment, I handed her the bag of fast-food, now in a grease-stained paper bag and no longer warm. She consumed the food like a ravenous dog having been starved. I was nervous and wanted to leave. There was no reason to be afraid of her; I was afraid *for* her. I was afraid of him. I wanted so badly to help her, yet I didn't know what to do. I was still a child.

Seeing her home for the first time, I was creeped out as I walked through the skeleton of an apartment, housing only the barest of essentials. A shell of a home, absent any personal belongings. Afraid of what I might see, I never looked into either bedroom and clearly understood that the need for a two-bedroom apartment was to turn tricks faster. My stomach churned, and I was moved to nausea as I looked at the bottle of mouthwash sitting on the bathroom sink.

It was a typical story. She moved to Denver from another state, with nothing, a low spot in her life. He targeted her. He helped her. He groomed her. Many young women trying to find their way often find themselves with no financial or emotional security and end up in precarious and dangerous situations. She was no exception.

My resources were limited. I was still in high school. Had I had the maturity to know whom to reach out to, I would have taken her to a women's shelter or the fire department.

I didn't have much, but I gave her the money that I had. As much as I wanted to help her, I could not bring this burden home to my family, to the instability of my own life. Above all, although she did not defend him, I knew that she would not leave him. Feeling no judgement for the path she had chosen, my ties with her must come to an end. This friendship could no longer continue. I needed to get out of the line of fire. I needed to avoid the mine field before me and walk away.

Having felt empathy for her, I knew—we both knew that we would never see each other again. We hugged goodbye, and I drove away in the drifting and blowing snow, shaken and trembling. Feeling empty and helpless, my heart was breaking for her. I was relieved to end this chapter of my journey into adulthood. My guardian angel watched over me that evening, as I pulled the car into my frozen driveway and safely returned home. I am meant to do more with my life.

I continued to encounter more forks in the road, enough to fill a hope chest. The policeman, in his dark uniform, just stood there shaking his head.

"I don't think you're cut out for this job. I think you should go find some other kind of work."

I had been selling cosmetics at the department store for a little over a year. Not only was I living on my own by now, but my younger sister had moved in with me, into a two-bedroom apartment. At just nineteen years old, I felt a responsibility to help her succeed in college, while she tried to overcome the challenges of poverty to become a first-generation college graduate. As much as I wanted to be in this line of work, $2.30 an hour did not leave a lot of wiggle room beyond making the monthly rent payment. The way to ensure a meal once the rent was paid was to have a second job, a night job in the food service industry.

The store detective stopped by the counter to chat, sharing with me her day.

"They're opening another store in the Aurora Mall. I can recommend you for the position. I can vouch for you."

Law enforcement had never occurred to me. It would not be something I would consider.

Yet…it paid $10 an hour. With a can of mace and a badge in hand, maybe I could be a store detective. How hard could it be?

The training consisted of a few bullet points: Do not make a false arrest. Wait for them to exit the store before apprehending them. Feel confident when you bring somebody into the office. Call the store manager for backup, and they will notify the mall police.

The most complicated part of my day was picking out my outfit. Look inconspicuous and catch someone stealing. I roamed the store, slithered up and down the aisles, trying to look like a shopper, but feeling like a sneak. There was pressure to apprehend the shoplifters. A quota. Surely someone is stealing something. How could a store justify hiring me if I never caught a thief? The irony of this position was that I hated to shop.

It was a boring routine, a lonely existence, day in and day out. And then one day it happened. The crime. A theft. An older man, maybe fifty years of age, and no more than 5 foot 8 inches, pilfering an item of clothing. Purloining a valuable item of merchandise. Perusing the items in the accessories department. A scarf. A little bit of nothing.

I waited for him to exit the store, feeling my adrenaline pumping. *Did he really just take that? A little old man. Am I nuts?* I had to convince myself. I wanted to make a rational decision. And then I made my move.

Pulling the security badge from my purse, I held it up at shoulder level and said, "Store security. I need to see your bag and your receipt. Please come with me."

"No, no, no. I bought it. I paid for it. I have the receipt."

"Show me your receipt. Is it in your pocket? Did you lose it?"

"I dropped it in the store."

"Show me where you paid for this. Which register?"

I wanted to believe him. I trusted everyone. I trusted this man was telling me the truth. I didn't want to believe that he did it. When I finally did catch a shoplifter, it broke my heart.

And as the mall police watched me interrogate this person, going from register to register to confirm that he did not pay for the scarf, looking throughout the store for the lost receipt, it became evidently clear that I was not cut out for this job. If a gang came through the store to grab a rack of leather coats, was I to stop them with just a can of mace? I don't think so. I realized the risk.

The armed policeman stood looking over my shoulder, shaking his head in disbelief, almost laughing out loud.

"You had him under surveillance. You saw him do it. You checked every way possible to confirm that he bought the scarf."

I went home that evening feeling very unsettled and with many thoughts. More than anything, I hated my job. Having been proud of myself for accomplishing the assignment, I knew I needed another job. A new occupation. It is my nature to trust people, so much so that I'm gullible. I am not cut out for loss prevention.

What I did learn from the experience was that it reaffirmed that makeup was my future, but that I needed to get better at it. It allowed me to interview for the downtown store and grow in my product knowledge. It taught me so much about security that I would use in my own business in years to come. Above all, I wanted to believe in humanity.

❧

Fast forward one year to 1976, one year following my high school graduation.

Yves St. Laurent, also known as YSL, was launching their new Opium fragrance line. They needed sales reps. I resurrected my navy-blue suit from the closet and met for the interview at the Colorado Mining Company, an upscale restaurant in Glendale, Colorado.

We spoke across the table, and I shared with a member of their management team my dreams and goals to be in the fashion and cosmetics industry. It was a reality check. Not only did he forgo the polite closing statements, "We'll get back to you," but he said, without hesitation, "You are not corporate material."

Looking back on this uphill journey to find my way, I have asked myself many times, why hadn't someone recommended cosmetology school? A guidance counselor, an employer, anyone along the way?

And so, I toiled in the department stores, piecemealing my life. I freelanced as a makeup artist, and along the way I began working for Chanel, on the floor of the department store, to promote new products. This allowed me to be in front of the counter and working directly with customers. It was like a duck to water, working with women and marketing products that I would select for them. I had not yet declared that "makeup" was my path, but it began to make sense. The pieces of the puzzle began to fit together.

During my short stint in college, I began volunteering in the theater department. I would also offer my makeup services to photographers, free of charge, to get experience with print work. I began selling Avon products in my spare time. Anything to learn.

After more time in the industry, the fog began to lift, and I had a vision. I knew what I wanted to do with my life. I wanted to be a makeup artist. If I say it over and over, out loud, it will have value and validity. "I am a makeup artist. I am a *professional* makeup artist." I was going to announce my career decision to my family at Easter dinner.

I sat at the dinner table in Lakewood, Colorado, among my many brothers and sisters and the ham and green bean casserole. My extended Italian family checks many of the boxes for stereotypical traits portrayed in movies. One brother pushed his food around the plate, burdened with the concept of "cleaning his plate." The other brother dished up his third helping, "just to be polite." As we laughed, argued, and overindulged in our meal, I proclaimed to my family that I was going to be a makeup artist.

"A makeup artist? What are you going to make up?"

"A make out artist?"

"Can you make a living at that?"

"Don't you have to go to cosmetology school?"

I explained that I was "grandfathered in," which allowed me to work without an esthetician's license. I could even go into cosmetology schools to teach, with my hundreds of hours of experience and training I had to undergo through repping the various lines, such as Lancome, Revlon, Ultima II, and Clinique.

While working for the different cosmetic lines, I began getting requests, and I was able to piece together twenty hours of work per week in the department stores. Yet, as any aspiring actor can confirm, I still had to wait tables at night to make ends meet.

One day, while working at the cosmetics counter in the department store, I was scouted by the founder of a local modeling school. She had heard good things about me and wanted me to come in to meet with her and discuss a job. I scheduled the time and date, made arrangements around my work schedule, and took public transit to get to the interview. Listening in the meeting, I learned more about her business, only to learn that she was offering me a receptionist position. I was insulted, quickly declined, and left feeling like I had wasted my morning.

A year later, she came into the department store to again offer me a job. I had now been with different cosmetic lines for about four years and had even more product knowledge.

"I'm not interested in an office job," I stated with conviction.

"No, no. This would be doing makeup."

The school was located in the heart of downtown Denver, a trendy area referred to as Larimer Square. It was an up-and-coming area for boutiques and salons, which at one time was home to brothels and houses of ill fame in the late 1800s. They needed someone to launch their curriculum and develop their product line. I thought, *Hell, I can do this!*

I was very proud of the program I put together; three courses in Basic Makeup, Photography Makeup, and Stage Makeup, and I was able to help them create their private label cosmetic line. I had holes in my shoes, I couldn't afford the parking, I would be paid straight commission, but I would be working doing something I loved. I had found my passion.

After two years of working for the modeling school, I needed a bigger pond, and I needed to make more money. I was tired of eating peanut butter and jelly sandwiches on white bread. While working with another manufacturer, repping and selling on the road in five different states, I was in and out of a hundred salons, makeup studios, modeling schools, department stores, private industry, and television stations. Every time I walked out of a building, I kept hearing myself say, *I can do better. It is so clear to me what is working and what needs to change.* I needed to work for myself. I needed to own my own studio.

I continued to stagnate in the cosmetics industry, yet I believed in what I was doing. I had taken the modeling school as far as I could and needed to move on and expand my horizons. Working as a sales representative for a cosmetics manufacturer, I began selling in the Colorado region, working on straight commission. No sales, no commission, no income. Working in the department stores was stifling. The need to expand my territory was the only way I was going to break this cycle. I would cover a five-state region: Arizona, California, Colorado, Texas, and Utah.

My plan began to unfold. I would liquidate everything I owned and live with my brother, in his guestroom. All I would need was my clothes. I would go on the road, not knowing how I was going to pay for it.

Before the Internet, there were two paths to access customers. The first was to obtain phone books from the library and make cold calls. No face-to-face meetings. Long distance phone calls at a time when you paid fees, by the minute, with no immediate access to customers. Cellular phones and unlimited long distance phone calls were still several decades into the future.

The second way to access customers was to travel to the city, rent a hotel room, get a local phone book, and start making cold calls and visits. I could not afford a rental car. My only mode of getting to appointments would have to be public transportation.

The process to liquidate everything I owned and earn some cash began. He needed a mattress. I needed $75. I had found a buyer, a bartender from a local restaurant.

It was a warm, clear day. I walked into the restaurant in Glendale, Colorado to collect the money from the sale of my mattress. My plan continued to evolve. The wheels in my head were racing like a wheel in a gerbil's cage as I spoke to myself, calculating the steps that needed to happen to go forward.

I walked back out of the restaurant with $75 closer to my objective, walking across the parking lot, atop the black asphalt and rows of striped pavement. My prayers continued, and I asked for help. *Dear God. Lord Jesus. Please. I know I'm supposed to do this. I just don't know how I'm going to pay for it.* I was driven by adrenaline. I was driven by fear. I was driven by hope. If there's a will, there's a way.

My white Subaru sat idle in the parking lot, amidst the cars belonging to patrons who could afford to eat at the restaurant. It was summer, and the heat radiated from the ground beneath my feet. At that time, all cars did not come fully equipped with air conditioning, and I dreaded stepping back into the heat of the car, which had been baking in the sun.

I pulled the car keys from my purse to unlock the car door. Something lying on the ground next to my automobile glinted and reflected the sunlight. It was a watch. A gold Lucien Piccard watch. I picked it up, feeling the weight of the timepiece in my hand. *Oh, my Lord. This looks real. I can't keep it. I've got to turn this into lost and found.* Knowing that someone would be very relieved to have this piece of jewelry returned, I walked back into the restaurant and left the watch with the bartender. He thanked me.

"If nobody comes and claims it, we'll call you," he replied matter-of-factly.

Somebody will come back and claim it. Surely. They will return to the restaurant and ask if anything had been turned in to lost and found. And yet, one week later, the event having slipped from my mind, I received a phone call. The watch was mine to keep.

Still not knowing whether the watch was valuable, or if it was real gold, I showed it to my mother, who worked in fine jewelry. She affirmed that it was valuable. I never took it in for a formal appraisal because I trusted her judgement.

We sat around the dinner table, replaying the story to my family. On the spot, my oldest brother opened his wallet and gave me $400. Cash. I had saved a few dollars and sold most of my belongings, but this windfall was my solution. This was the answer to my prayers. This was my airline ticket and hotel for my first job. I'm headed to San Diego. This is what I'm supposed to do. This is my destiny.

Bill and Hillary Clinton - 1999

"Mutual Respect"

This was my fourth occasion to meet one of the Clintons. The first occasion was in Dallas, Texas when the very young and charismatic Bill Clinton was running for president. The second time was in 1993, after Bill had secured the presidency and Hillary was speaking on behalf of healthcare reform. The third event was our highly sought after and anticipated interview in Moscow with Bill Clinton in 1994. And the most memorable was this interview for *60 Minutes II*, shrouded by the Columbine High School shooting in Littleton, Colorado and following the impeachment scandal with President Clinton. As I prepared my kit in the hotel room, I felt that time, once again, had repeated itself.

The Columbine massacre took place on April 20, 1999, in which two high school seniors killed twelve students, one teacher, injured more than twenty others, and finally turned the gun fatally on themselves. Dan Rather was in Littleton to cover the story, which would air the following week. One of several camera crews to be taking footage, along with Bill and Hillary Clinton, were in town to recognize the one-month anniversary of the Columbine tragedy and speak at the observance.

I had taken a commercial flight to my home state of Colorado, staying in a moderately priced hotel just off I-25. It felt oddly strange to fly home and cover a national story of this magnitude, just a few miles from my own high school. It was spring, with very little evidence of the remnants of winter. Dan stood on the dormant grass, with the view of Columbine High School in the distance. The area was cordoned off with yellow crime scene tape. Throngs of people were in the area, both on foot and in cars, and brought mountains of flowers, stuffed animals, and memorabilia to leave at the make-shift memorial. Personal belongings of the young students still lay inside the high school, waiting for confirmation that all explosive devices had been secured. The mood was heavy and somber, almost palpable.

President Bill Clinton and First Lady Hillary Clinton both spoke at Dakota Ridge High School to address the Columbine student body and their families, but Ms. Clinton had agreed to meet with Dan Rather, individually, later that same day. The very public and long, drawn out impeachment of President Clinton had concluded just a few months prior, and Hillary Clinton had yet to speak publicly with the press. The impeachment had been front and center in the headline news for over a year. It was an honor for Dan to secure this interview. It was an understanding of mutual respect. Dan honored the sanctity of marriage and Hillary's right to privacy; Hillary knew that Dan would treat the topic with the utmost dignity and solemnity.

This was a double-header for CBS. First, the Columbine story, followed by an interview with Hillary Clinton. We had a "fluid" schedule; in other words, no idea when the interview would occur. Once it was evident that the ceremony would be prolonged and the window for opportunity to get the interview was narrowing, CBS began to strategize a plan. The Secret Service would safely and time-ly get Ms. Clinton the almost forty miles to Denver International Airport, but we had to contend with Denver rush hour traffic.

When it was clear that time was running out, CBS scrambled to charter a private helicopter to take four or five of us to DIA. One of the producers informed us that we had secured our transportation. We could not risk missing this opportunity due to something as trivial as traffic.

The chopper landed on the grass, its massive blades swirling, the volume of the engine championing its arrival. I was lugging my makeup kit across the grass and parking lot to board the aircraft. I could feel my heart begin to pound and accelerate, and I began to get a bit anxious, as my symptoms of motion sickness began to appear. Sometimes it is subtle and can be managed with over-the-counter medication; sometimes not so much. But due to the uncertainty of our day, I did not know about the helicopter ride and had not taken the medication, not to mention that by this time it was too late. The medication would not have had time to take effect.

I recall a conversation with Dan at one time in which he asked me, "Do you have a fear of flying?" He perceived it as anxiety. I responded with my sarcastic sense of wit, "No, I have a fear of throwing up!"

We boarded the helicopter, and I found my seat towards the back of the cabin. Once again, my choice of words tumbled out before thinking it through, and I heard myself asking, "Are we supposed to have a parachute?"

We were given headsets to wear, which allowed us to talk to each other and communicate with the pilot, as well. As we're moving northeast through the city to the airport, the pilot shares with us that there is a hailstorm coming and that we need to go around it. It was clearly visible from our vantage point, very isolated, almost like a dark gray cylinder in the sky, and he was going to maneuver around it. Not to worry.

What I also recall about our excursion is that we were very low to the ground. I think I would have felt safer in an airplane. It was my first encounter in a helicopter, and although I was battling with motion sickness, I recall that the skyline and city were very beautiful. I had never viewed the Mile High City quite like this.

As I looked down upon the interstates lined with cars, I could fully appreciate why CBS made the decision to fly the friendly skies. To my great relief, we had a very skilled pilot and except for the liftoff and landing, the transport did not prove challenging.

After landing at DIA, we were met by a driver and car and escorted to a private entrance leading to a conference room. Although I'm sure the room was already "swept" by the Secret Service, we were able to avoid the lines through security and conveyor belts scanning our possessions. Looking out through the large windows of the conference room onto the tarmac were Airforce I and Airforce II, what I jokingly refer to as the "He/She" airplanes.

I greeted the First Lady, and to my surprise she was travelling with three or four female companions, what I will call "her armor." They were very protective of her, until I introduced myself as the makeup artist. Then I felt the tension in the room begin to loosen. I can only imagine that this was a sensitive interview, knowing that despite the events involving Columbine High School, the impeachment scandal would certainly be broached. To discuss a personal betrayal and the hurt in her heart was difficult enough, not to mention all of the baggage and exploitation that followed the story.

Hillary was dressed very classically—a dark suit adorned with a braided gold rope necklace and coordinating earrings. She sat down for me to apply her makeup, and I inquired whether there were any specific requests. She replied simply that she trusted my judgement. I knew that I wanted to keep her makeup natural and conservative. Dan wanted to welcome her and greet her, and he was already in makeup. He never wanted to have me fussing over him in front of a guest. Likewise, he was not present when I applied her makeup. It would not have been considered gentlemanly, almost as if it were a dressing room. It was that of mutual respect.

Once underway with the interview, I looked on, watching the skilled journalism of Dan and the composure and grace of the First Lady. To her credit, she stood her ground on topics that were personal, and left inquiry of the President's indiscretions for her husband to answer. I marveled at the dignified presence of both professionals. Mutual respect.

Presidential Candidate Bill Clinton, August 1992

Presidential Class Photo, January 14, 1994. Courtesy: Sharon Farmer, photographer, William J. Clinton Presidential Library

Hillary Clinton - *60 Minutes II*
Healthcare Reform
https://danratherjournalist.org/investigative-journalist/60-minutes-ii/
hillary-clinton/video-1993-hillary-clinton-interview

One-year Anniversary of Columbine High School Shooting
https://danratherjournalist.org/investigative-journalist/60-minutes-ii/
hillary-clinton/video-1999-hillary-clinton-interview

LuAnn Mancini - 1984

"The Studio—a Wing and a Prayer"

He walked up to the front door and knocked unabashedly. The woman opened the door, questioning who the stranger on her front porch might be.

"Do you have any interest in selling your home? I'd like to talk with you about buying it."

And in another serendipitous moment, he discovered that he knew her brother. They were friends. He had taken a class with him at University of Texas—Arlington. The negotiations began. She had been thinking about selling, she was ready to move, and she would carry the note on the loan for five years.

I first met Marion at the stockyards in the historic district of Fort Worth. I had been on the road and staying with friends, making sales calls in the Dallas/Fort Worth market. It was the celebration of the Chisholm Trail, and it was hard to know what was real and what was a performance. The long-horned cattle ambled down the center of East Exchange Avenue, their hooves sounding like the soundtrack from a cowboy western. The massive beasts did not appear to be having as much fun as the crowds that cheered them on. The cowboys rode atop their dapple horses, looking out from underneath their Stetson hats, enjoying the attention. The facades of the buildings retained their original hand-forged brick. There were no bars, just saloons, and the sidewalks were crowded with people ready to celebrate.

My friend and I were in the dance hall, enjoying the live music. We stood alongside the rail of the dance floor watching the crowd. It was apparent who the locals were, skillfully maneuvering on the crowded dance floor, and who the tourists were, just hoping for a line dance.

He came up to my friend and asked her to dance; he loved music. I wasn't his type. He stood out like a sore thumb in his khaki slacks and blue, button-down shirt, very much looking like an architect.

"No, thank you," she replied. He wasn't her type. She wasn't going to waste the time.

"Well, would *you* like to dance?" he said to me, more a statement than a question.

"Yes, I'll dance!" I said, looking forward to the country swing that was currently playing on the loud, overhead speakers.

We began to talk. He had recently immigrated from Warsaw, Poland and had only been in the United States for four or five years. I was fascinated by his journey. I'm a sucker for an accent. Once he started to speak, I knew I was in trouble. We danced, we talked, we dated, we fell in love.

It was clear to me that Texas was a stronger market for the makeup industry. The 1980s was a time of big hair, big shoulder pads, and glamour. The wildly popular television show *Dallas* was at its peak.

When I made the decision to walk away from the clients in Colorado and an investor to freelance in Texas, Marion offered to help me move and find an apartment. When he came to Colorado to load the car, he proposed.

On a wing and a prayer and $50,000, my dream began to take shape. He was on a hunt. He knew zoning, he knew architecture, he knew Fort Worth. It was clear to Marion what I needed. A free-standing building, not a lease in a strip mall. "It needs to be on the Westside, old money, where the clientele can support your business. It needs to be convenient, on the edge of a residential area where it can be zoned commercial." He imagined more than what I saw. All I wanted was a full book of appointments and to be paid what I felt I was worth. He knew my dreams were too small. "You will grow into this space, and then you will outgrow this space."

I walked into the small, two-bedroom, one-bath, wood-framed house at 5017 Byers Avenue. Paint swatches covered the walls in gray, peach, aqua, and blue.

"Which color is it going to be?" I asked him.

"All of them," he boasted.

"Really? All in this building?" He imagined more than I saw.

We embraced the art deco elements of the home, and the dated exterior of the brown and white structure with Western shutters became a cottage of pink, white, and mauve. An overgrown tree in the front yard was removed to create a circle drive. I borrowed $1,000 to purchase my first order of cosmetics. And on the third attempt, the commercial zoning was granted. After a few years in business, with all the loans coming due, my lucky stars continued to align, and I qualified for an SBA loan. The forks in the road began to merge into a clear path.

5017 Byers Avenue - Ft. Worth, Texas

Local news interview.

Architectural Design: Marion Zygadlo

Wendell Abbott - 1984

"The Prankster"

"Is it beef?"

We were seated at a table, amidst the abundance of wood, red and white checkered tablecloths, and deep-fried appetizers.

The waitress at the Northside steakhouse placed the dish onto the center of the table between the two of us. The mound of crispy pieces, enough for a serving of four, looked very inviting. The display of what appeared to be breaded mushrooms surrounded an enticing pool of ranch dressing.

"Yes, it's beef. Have one," he said to me with a twinkle in his eye. The corners of his mouth turned up slightly in a small smirk as our eyes met. I sliced off a small bite of the appetizer with a fork and knife and placed the sampling into my mouth. It was flavorful, yet Wendell was not to be trusted. Something about the texture was different. I swallowed, not knowing what to think. He openly laughed, unable to contain himself.

"They're bull's testicles!"

At that moment, I wasn't sure whether I was going to be able to keep my food down. Madder than a hornet at Wendell, I wanted to kill him. Apparently in Texas, the Rocky Mountain oysters of Colorado are called "calf fries."

Wendell was a prankster, never taking anyone, or himself, too seriously, always wanting to keep people guessing. He took pride in living in the moment, and he valued and treasured close friendships, looking after those he cared for most deeply. We became colleagues, compadres, and cherished companions over the span of twenty years.

I first met Wendell at the Miss Texas pageant in 1984. It was 5:30 a.m. during pageant week, earlier than most humans are awake. He was a very handsome man, with a thick mop of wavy, brunette hair. His frame was tall and lean, probably due to his smoking habit. He had an engaging smile, and he carried himself with an air of assurance. Wendell caught the eye of both men and women in the industry. I entered the hotel to find him surrounded by four or five women, what appeared to be a harem of contestants dressed in bathrobes. They were seated around him as he leisurely brushed and teased their hair, occasionally taking time to savor his coffee with his free hand.

If ever there were two opposites, we were it. He was the official hairdresser; I was the official makeup artist for the pageant. He was male; I was female. He moved very intentionally and did not rush; I moved like a bull in a China shop. While he was well known in the pageant world, I was new on the scene, yet the owner of a business. He watched as I entered and consumed the room, hyperactive and sweaty, opening every window that I could to bring in more direct light. He worked calmly with each young woman in his chair; I had several contestants booked at fifteen-minute intervals, needing them to stand as I applied their makeup. I thought to myself, *What in the world? He is never going to get to all of those women. What is he thinking?*

The first item on the agenda was the pageant interviews. After the initial flurry of excitement and preparation, there is always a lot of down time. While the "girls" were meeting with a panel of judges, the tech and backstage crew could take a moment to decompress. This is when I came to learn that he worked at a salon but was still building his business and needed clientele.

Success leads to more success, and over the course of time we became each other's best source of referrals. I would send him hair clients, and he would return the favor to me. Within a short, two-year period, we had both stabilized our careers. Regardless of what time I called him, he would always make himself available, and I was needing to hire and train new makeup artists to meet the demand at the studio. He was grateful and thankful for the work, and I ultimately became one of his clients. Our friendship grew, and he became one of my closest confidants.

On my days off, Wendell would "kidnap" me. He intuitively sensed my level of stress and would "casually" drop by to take me to lunch. Unknowingly, I would find myself on all-day adventures, Wendell unwilling to return me to my home. One of his favorite outings was visiting graveyards. He found beauty in the tombstones and the grounds of the cemetery and was well versed in history, so much so that he became my personal docent. He loved to explore, and I found myself with no choice. He had the car, he was driving, and I had to surrender my to-do list waiting for me at home. Early in my career, he was one of the few people I would trust to be seen without makeup. In the world of fashion and beauty, it is a facade and reputation that I felt I had to maintain. Wendell allowed me to be me.

We spent many days at Lake Worth. Wendell leased a rental property on the northeast side of the lake near Carswell Naval Air Station, which allowed us to watch the sunsets to the west. I called it "the cottage," but really it was a large lot for a one-bedroom. Alongside the rental property sat an old wooden dock, a few feet above the water's surface. Because the cottage sat up on a bluff, and the lake and dock were down below, removed from view, it felt like we were in the country—yet just a few miles from the hustle and bustle of Fort Worth and still inside the city limits. The dilapidated garage that sat on the property added to the country charm.

Wendell would fish, and I would swim. It was a poor man's vacation that made you feel rich, inside and out. I would return home feeling a reprieve from the chaos of my work and hectic schedule. It was a friendship that many envied. At the same time, people questioned the platonic nature of our relationship.

Wendell knew he was not going to live a long life. Regardless of what he wanted to hear or believe, his doctors were very candid with him. He would never find himself in a nursing home, a shell of himself. A genetic heart condition took his mother when he was just a young boy, and he inherited the genetic condition. It would be swift and unpredictable.

If he wanted to prolong his life, he would need to stop smoking, exercise, stop eating chicken fried steak, and live a healthier lifestyle. As though he waved his finger in the face of danger, he refused. He smoked like a train and would live life to the fullest, truth be damned. When God comes to call, he will be ready.

Miss Texas, Miss USA, Miss America - 1985–1996
Gretchen Carlson
Life Magazine - "The Sting"

It was like bees to honey. The more women I encountered, and the more "pageant winners" I added to my client list, the faster I became known in the industry as the "makeup guru" (*Pageantry Magazine*).

For those unfamiliar with the process, women must first enter a pageant at the local level and win in order to compete in Miss Texas. They can then go on to try to become Miss Texas, then Miss USA or Miss America. From 1985 through 1997, every contestant who won the Miss Texas pageant was "one of my girls."

Miss Texas
1985 Miss Greenville
1986 Miss Grand Prairie
1987 Miss Greenville
1988 Miss Duncanville
1989 Miss Haltom-Richland Area
1990 Miss Humble/Kingwood
1991 Miss Lake O' The Pines
1992 Miss Tarrant County
1993 Miss Northeast Texas
1994 Miss Amarillo
1995 Miss Oak Cliff
1996 Miss Dallas

1997 Miss Lake O' The Pines
1999 Miss Hurst-Euless-Bedford

Miss USA
1987, 1988, 1989

Miss America
1989, 1990, 1996

From that first moment after getting the crown pinned to her hair when she becomes Miss Texas, I would coach, guide, and sponsor her for the Miss America contest. The pageant is, in itself, an extremely stressful day—full of emotion, spotlights, sweat, and tears. Once Miss Texas is crowned and swept backstage, I would swoop in and touch up her makeup for the first post-pageant TV interview. The following day is typically the first photo shoot and headshot for promotional material.

Over the course of the year, I then guide her through an advanced makeup lesson for both interview makeup and stage makeup, and then supply cosmetics for the entirety of her reigning year. It was always very exciting for my clients to see "Miss Texas" in the studio and shop alongside her. Leah Kay Lyle, Miss Texas 1990, would come into the studio and ask apologetically if it was okay to park the Miss Texas automobile out front. "You betcha. Park it right up front where everyone can see it!" If you're wondering why Miss Texas always looks so beautiful, it's not an accident. It takes a lot of hard work and attention to detail.

While some might view this as purely a successful career, I truly got to know these young women and would do whatever I could to help make their dreams come true. On one such trip home to Colorado, I was helping my family with a garage sale and liquidation of personal property. Miss Colorado was so eager to meet with me that she agreed to come to the garage sale, and we slipped away to the back bedroom to have a makeup lesson amidst the chaos of the bargains being sold on the front lawn.

Texas had become a "mecca," so to speak, because Miss Texas has placed in the top ten of the Miss America pageant almost thirty times in the last forty years. The Dallas/Fort Worth area was also known for people who were legends in their field—custom designed gowns, swimsuits, personal trainers, and now, after a growing list of winners in the pageants, makeup. Women were coming to Fort Worth to meet with me for lessons and my expertise. In 1989, I had the privilege of working with Gretchen Carlson.

After winning the Miss Anoka and Miss Minnesota competition, Gretchen flew into Fort Worth to have makeup lessons with me. I saw her on two different occasions. She was a perfectionist in every way, detail oriented, and makeup was no different. I recall her telling me, "I'm not a pageant person. This will be my first year, and this will be my only year." She was in it to win.

What I found most astonishing, astounding really, was that the more beautiful the woman, the more talented the woman, the higher the bar. The "girls" were always their own worst critics. While in my studio, during a makeup lesson, she shared with me a story about her grandpa. They had a close bond, a tight family unit. He affectionately referred to her as "Sparkles." He said to her that she could never become Miss America; she was too short.

For those of you that don't know this, Gretchen is only 5'3". It's very unusual for pageant winners to be under 5'8" or even 5'10", very similar to the modeling industry. Gretchen had the beauty, the poise and grace, the intelligence, the confidence, and the talent. She was the valedictorian of her high school, educated and an honor student at Stanford, studied at Oxford University, and studied violin at the Juilliard School of Music. Miss America, look no further. There was no reason that she couldn't be the first 5'3" Miss America. Let's prove them wrong.

The talent portion of the competition accounts for 50 percent of a contestant's score. With fifty-one performances to be judged, they are spread out over three days. Because the talent competition is weighted so heavily, the three winners from the talent competition are a shoo-in for the top-ten finalists.

In the early days, we were allowed to do makeup for contestants on the day of a competition, but makeup artists were never allowed backstage. A contestant must do their own makeup at the convention center hall, but it was not uncommon for me to be hired prior to the actual competition

At 7:00 a.m., the morning following her talent competition, I went to Gretchen's hotel room to do her makeup for the day. I was greeted at the door, and I was invited into the room. Gretchen was not herself. It appeared she had been crying. I began to set up my kit and cosmetics, and she began to open up.

"I can play it so much better. I can play it so much better, and I will for the finals, on Saturday night."

I thought to myself, *I don't understand. I thought she won the competition.* She had, in fact, won the talent competition the previous evening. Perfectionist and driven, first and foremost. When I "coached" the girls with their makeup, I always tried to instill a sense of inner self, to help them see their own inner beauty and bring out their confidence. When Gretchen walked into a room, she came in, package intact, the whole deal. The violin was her "secret weapon," but this sense of self would certainly help her advance to the top ten.

We went to work. Everything down to the last detail was orchestrated and scheduled on a tightly timed agenda. Within a short time, she was ready to go—no longer any remains of what she may have been feeling. Because I had already worked with Gretchen on two different occasions, we customized products chosen especially for her. In the '80s, the options were fewer than today, such as the gel eye liner and certain types of matte eye shadow. To say that all products were waterproof, or should I say tear proof, would not be accurate. Gretchen was tough and would hold up under the pressure. Hopefully, if there was watershed, it would be because she had won!

When I say that the bar was high, what most women would consider the height of their accomplishments—winning the Miss America pageant—was only the beginning for Gretchen, as you may know. Fox News Anchor, journalist, actress, women's rights activist, and published author, from which I quote:

"Each morning before I left the hotel, I had my makeup done, because the makeup artists weren't allowed in the hall. I had brought in a fabulous lady named LuAnn Mancini, a talented Texan whose claim to fame was that she did Dan Rather's makeup—which shows her range. LuAnn was a delight and something of a genius. She had perfected an airbrushing technique, long before it was in common use in TV studios" (Gretchen Carlson, *Getting Real,* pg. 100).

I apologize if I have misstated Gretchen's words in my retelling of the story. I am flattered to have been mentioned in Gretchen's memoirs.

The Miss America pageant brought a huge influx of people to Atlantic City: pageant contestants, their families, tourists, and the press. This filled hotel rooms, restaurants, gambling casinos, taxi-cabs, etc. Even the parade held on Friday night requires a ticket. It means tens of millions of dollars to the city.

Because all the big-name hotels wanted representation and to be able to host the pageant contestants—and with it, bragging rights—the girls were staying at many different hotels along the boardwalk. Marquees are draped across the facades of the buildings, proudly publicizing which contestants are staying at their hotel.

Logistically, because the girls were at many hotels, oftentimes I was racing from hotel to hotel for my tightly booked appointments. Because of this, I could only book four contestants during one pageant and slotted their makeup sessions for forty-five-minute intervals. During the afternoon break, I would then return and make my rounds again, to touch up their makeup.

I was in the audience that evening to see Gretchen crowned Miss America 1989. That wasn't always the case, to see other contestants compete. One year my assistant was with me, and we were so run ragged that we opted to stay in the hotel room for the televised finals of the Miss America Pageant. Imagine that! Years of training for these young women, personal ties to many, the excitement and the drama of the finals, and we opted to stay at the hotel. So, there we were in full makeup, in our beaded evening gowns with our feet up on the bed, watching on the television screen with our Caesar salads. It was what the industry demanded of us. We mused that we had the best seats in the house. After the thrill of the crowning, we did attend the after party. That's when I got my bragging rights. When one of my girls won, I felt as though I had won, too!

Once word got out that I could help young women achieve their goals and dreams as a beauty pageant winner, I then began getting calls from young female equestrians hoping to become Rodeo Queens.

In a September 29, 2000 interview by News On 6, Kendall Morgan says:

"Makeup artist LuAnn Mancini's work with three Miss Americas and three Miss USAs led her to the rodeo queens."

I am quoted as saying, "They need to have something they can do quickly in their trailer, and they need to be able to do it without water. It's not truly theatrical makeup, but it's borderline. I would work with one or two…a year, the cream of the crop, who've had some custom clothes made and some special saddles. It's very expensive, so by the time they find me, they're pretty serious about winning."

When I say that I truly got to know these young women and would do whatever I could to help make their dreams come true, others did not always feel the same. In 1993, I was called by the *The Maury Povich Show* to appear as part of a panel. They were doing a show on beauty pageants, which are oftentimes known for getting a lot of bad press. Opponents to beauty pageants argue that they diminish the value of women, they objectify women, women were made to be ornaments or trophies, and other less politically correct verbiage.

I initially declined, not wanting to be a part of the sensationalism and shock value of the show. The associate on the phone assured me that this was going to be a different kind of program, to demonstrate the value of the scholarships and the positive impact pageants can have on young women. The panel was to include professionals in the pageant world, such as gown designers, hairdressers, trainers, and even a plastic surgeon. I was asked to participate to represent makeup artists. We all catered to this industry and were known "to win."

After being assured this was not a show to denigrate the industry, I agreed to appear on the show, as did the other members on the panel. We were all in hopes of getting some good exposure and good press, and we all showed up with our best game.

After a brief introduction of the panel and a "polite" synopsis of the show, Maury began down the rabbit hole. He asked, "What is the ideal?" The swimsuit designer was questioned on the practice of using spray glue on women's buttocks to keep a swimsuit from riding up. The plastic surgeon was asked about liposuction and cosmetic surgery.

When it was my turn, I was asked about the use of Preparation H on a woman's face, typically used on hemorrhoids. My response was, "I don't know, Maury. You will have to ask someone who uses that technique." He quickly rebounded and said, "Okay, what is the premise?" I responded that the theory was that the Preparation H reduced inflammation and swelling and that it was used to reduce puffiness under someone's eyes.

The plastic surgeon went on to defend his position, that he had performed a rhinoplasty on a singer for a deviated septum, to help aid her breathing.

As a panel, we were brought there to discredit beauty pageants and produce a seedy show, and we weren't going to allow it. We argued that while contestants have different reasons for participating in pageants, women would seek out the aid of professionals whether they participated in pageants or not; they have issues about themselves that they wish to improve upon.

At one point, I pointed out that makeup was used to make you "camera ready." From the audience you are able to see a person's features on stage. Under harsh lighting, a person is not washed out. I said, "Like the makeup you have on your face right now, Maury." That remark was edited from the final broadcast.

In August of 1990, lightning again attempted to strike. Because Texas was gaining so much notoriety in the pageant circles, an article was going to be written up in *Life* magazine. I received a phone call from Jeannie Ralston, one of their journalists. She was going to do a story on B. Don Magness, chairman of the board and a man well known in the industry of the Miss Texas pageant. "We're going to be in town. Can we come in to take photos of your studio?"

I thought it was a very insightful way to understand the process, to follow contestants around and get a better idea of how they go about preparing for a pageant. The article was timed perfectly. She was in town for the week of the Miss Texas pageant, and Miss America would take place in September. She wanted to spend a day at the studio, take photos, and watch me work.

Wow, I thought. *This is a big deal. This is coverage in* Life *magazine! Women are going to come from every state for me.* I was very excited and thrilled to have her there for the day. I didn't know whether I was going to get a paragraph or a page, but to be interviewed for *Life* magazine was momentous.

Jeannie came with the photographer and spent a good part of the day in my studio. We didn't stray from the topic of makeup into other areas of pageant preparation. She was very good at her job, about getting information, costs associated with makeup, what it would take to prepare a contestant, videotaping at the time of the lesson, and before and after photos. She picked my brain. She did not venture from that topic.

Over the course of the week, Jeannie continued to accumulate information. She was at all rehearsals and stayed with the schedule. I didn't know how the story was going to unfold, but I knew that B. Don was the feature because Texas had had so many winners.

As it turns out, and what I didn't know at the time, the article was what I would call a sting, digging up dirt. It was an investigative story to see why the numbers were so skewed towards Texas.

The *Life* magazine article came out in September of 1990. It was a full four pages. After the article went to print, June Mirike, the president of the Miss Texas pageant, came by the studio.

I greeted her with enthusiasm and asked, "How does it look? Good article? Good coverage?" She looked white. The color seemed to wash from her face.

"Oh, LuAnn. This is bad. They did not mention you, but this is something you don't want to be a part of." For this I will remain forever thankful to Jeannie Ralston.

After June Mirike left the studio, I immediately went out to purchase a copy. Anticipating the worst, I knew it was going to be not only bad, but really bad.

The article opened with a full-page photograph of B. Don in a hot tub with a cigar, quoted as saying, "Come on in, sluts." It was vulgar, shining a different light on pageants. It touched on controlling the women, manipulation, discrimination, and what I would call inappropriate behavior towards the contestants. The article was not at all what I thought it was going to be, nor do I think B. Don Magness thought it was going to be that kind of article. While portions of the article focused on B. Don's involvement and trajectory of the contestants leading to pageant winners, Jeannie was a journalist who often wrote on behalf of women and did not find "Good Ol' Boy" humor funny. Quite the contrary. These were very young, impressionable girls, some as young as eighteen years of age. The oldest contestants were just twenty-three.

After a thirty-year association and a two-month investigation, Mr. Magness resigned as pageant director of the Miss Texas pageant.

Later, he was forced to resign as a board member. There was no wrongdoing on my part. I always had the best interests of the girls in mind and always tried to operate ethically. Some might say that any press is good press; I would strongly disagree. Any association with this article would have been devastating to my business, my studio, my reputation, and my name. Whether you call it the grace of God, good fortune, living a clean life, or just plain Karma, I had dodged a bullet.

You may read further about the stories detailed in this chapter in the following publications:

How to Win Pageants – Ginie Polo Sayles; Wordware Publishing 1989
The Magic of Makeup: Talking with LuAnn Mancini

Pageantry Magazine - Holiday Issue 1992
From Pageant to Prom
https://www.worthpoint.com/worthopedia/
pageantry-magazine-1992-justin-510227049

***Getting Real*, Penguin Random House - Gretchen Carlson**
Miss America Crowning 1989 - Gretchen Carlson
https://www.youtube.com/watch?v=zNiaD7MB3N8

Miss America Talent Competition 1989 - Gretchen Carlson
https://www.youtube.com/watch?v=w19oF6c3kJk

Dallas Morning News - September 29, 2000, 12:00 a.m.
News On 6 - Kendall Morgan
http://www.newson6.com/story/5e36848d2f69d76f62099ba6/
rodeo-queens:-for-madonna-the-look-is-just-another-
fling-but-to-others-it-has-a-deeper-meaning

Life Magazine, September 1990 – Ellis Island
Mr. Miss Texas; B. Don Magness
https://2neat.com/product/life-magazine-september-1990-ellis-island/

Washington Post, November 1990
https://www.washingtonpost.com/archive/lifestyle/1990/11/22/
pageant-member-ousted/627fff38-140a-46ac-acca-6827a203f0c6/

Wendell Abbott - 1980s

"Jewel Charity Ball"

It was a ball that even Cinderella could not have imagined. The Jewel Charity Ball earned its reputation as one of the major fundraisers for the Cook Children's Hospital, with charity angels from every walk of life wearing their best finery. Floor length ball gowns in every shade of the rainbow were on display, with gallantly dressed men on the arm of the guests and debutantes. The theme of the ball varies from year to year, but "The Jewel" was not to be missed!

The theme for this year's ball was New Orleans Mardi Gras. I had known Wendell for a few years. He had phoned at the last minute to ask me if I wanted to join him; he had been invited and was going to go. I don't recall which words he used, but would I like to join him for his plus-one?

Like Cinderella, I would be working all day, with back-to-back appointments for the women that would be attending the ball and had booked me, and then miraculously need to pull myself together for the ball. Wendell was convincing, and it sounded like fun. I thought, *Why not?* We often donated to this type of charity. Sometimes we would create a package gift certificate for hair and makeup. *It will be prestigious to make an appearance, see all of our clients, and have a nice meal and a drink.*

I didn't give it much more thought, other than trying to figure out what to wear. I combed through my closet and came up with a 3/4 length black skirt, a silver off-the-shoulder top, black cocktail shoes, and a silver bando in my hair. With full makeup and my mane of curls billowing out of the top, I could make it work.

Wendell was old school Texan, through and through. He believed in church on Sundays, graveyards, and Cadillacs. He picked me up at my home, and he looked quite dashing in his tux. We made our way to the ball and pulled up behind limousines and chauffeur-driven automobiles, arriving fashionably late. We left the Cadillac with the valet and made our way to the red carpet.

I was taking it all in and didn't pay much attention to the host, who was greeting guests and welcoming donors. Wendell was greeted by our client, and he checked us in.

We began to mingle and make our way through the crowd with 1200 of our closest friends. The event was in full swing, with live music, jugglers, face painting, and a car being raffled to raise money for the Children's Hospital. Partygoers were wearing beautifully designed masks covered in jewels, feathers, and beads. Everyone was covered from head to toe in custom-made costumes, predominantly in a theme of green, purple, and gold. Alcohol was flowing. The energy was electric. It was where you wanted to be if you were "somebody."

It took us an hour to get through the crowd, and by this time I was ready for a drink. He said, "Just wait here. I'll get us a drink." Wendell returned with drinks, and I began to look around, wondering where our seats were. *Where is our table?* After a long day, now I'm ready to get off my feet. Now I'm ready to sit down and have a meal. By now it's 9:30 or 10:00 p.m. I asked, "Where is our table? Where are our seats?"

Wendell turned to me with the same expression as when he'd tricked me into eating calf fries, that same ornery grin, and said, "We don't have any seats. We can sit at any one of these tables we would like, but we don't have assigned seats."

I said, "What? We don't have tickets?"

He said, "No, we didn't need tickets. The chairperson was our client."

"We need to eat. Did we crash—"

"We did not crash—"

"We crashed the Jewel Charity Ball!"

"No, we were *invited* to the Jewel Charity Ball. Not all of these seats are going to be used."

"Oh, my gosh, Wendell!"

My mind began to race, and I began to look around, as though a child caught with their hand in the cookie jar. What if someone comes back, and we're sitting in their seats? I was still early in my career as a business owner, not wanting to make mistakes. It brought me back to childhood, where you were not invited to a party, but you got to peek in. There was a beautiful buffet set up, but you were only allowed to look. Don't touch. It's not for you. What if my clients found out I'd crashed the Jewel Charity Ball? It brought back insecurity, even though I knew we could afford to eat anywhere we wanted.

"I am hungry, and I want to sit down and eat, and I am not going to go get a plate of food at the buffet."

"Okay. Let's go across the street and eat and we can come back."

So there we were, sitting in formal wear at Juanita's, with Wendell and my chili relleno.

We were extremely overdressed, and people would walk by and wonder, trying not to overtly gawk. I did not attend another Jewel Charity ball again. The excitement was over. I never told any of my clients. I felt too exposed.

Wendell, the prankster, had pulled one over on me, unconcerned about what people might think. He would live in the moment and live life to the fullest. When God comes to call, he will be ready.

Tiananmen Square; Beijing, China - May 1989
"History Unfolding"

Never knowing when my phone would ring, when that might be, I looked forward to the travel and the excitement, the fast pace of the changing news cycles, and I always welcomed that next story. At times it would be weeks, even months, in between calls. At other times, there would be a phone message waiting for me upon my return from a job I had just completed for CBS. But once you get a taste for it—the excitement of the cameras, the lights, the live broadcasts, the adrenaline—you're "hooked." And by this time, the news crew were my friends, colleagues, and family.

Newsstands and grocery store checkout aisles are littered with magazines, detailing the exploits of the rich and famous. Celebrities yearn for public attention, recognition, the ongoing fame, the elusive spotlight, and perfecting their craft. Fans who purchase these publications are equally engrossed in following their lives, almost as though they are a part of it. I can only imagine the same could be said about any profession, really—chasing your dream, the next big client, the next project, the next job offer. To say that I didn't look forward to the next time I was called to be on a job, on location, would be untrue.

I was able to witness the cry for liberty and reform, the protests of young and hopeful students, the stifling blow of the government, and the aftermath. The Tiananmen Square demonstration was without question the most memorable and impactful event in my thirty-five-year career as a makeup artist.

It started as a straightforward job: foreign leaders planning to meet with other foreign leaders, doing what foreign leaders do. Mikhail Gorbachev was to meet with members of the Chinese government, an unprecedented summit that hadn't occurred since 1959. History was unfolding. I got the phone call to travel with CBS to Beijing for this story. *Okay. Fun. This will be fun,* I thought naively.

As I began the preparations for the trip, the list was endless. Passport, travel clothing, my makeup kit, backups to my makeup kit, and backups to the backups. By now my makeup kit had undergone many evolutions, to bigger and better. Compartments and drawers filled with brightly colored lipsticks, foundations in every skin tone, brushes, cotton swabs, and sponges. It was all-encompassing.

I always chuckled to myself when going through customs, waiting for the agent to open the lid and peer inside. It was very predictable. The tackle box moves smoothly through the x-ray scanner. I am quietly asked to step out of line and step away from the conveyor belt. Gloved hands open and examine the contents inside. The look on the faces of the TSA representative was always that of bewilderment and surprise when looking at the array of tubes, canisters, and bottles, expecting to see lures, hooks, and feathers. Priceless.

Today, as I now think of the airline regulations and restrictions since 9/11, this would be a more difficult feat. I can't imagine the pastes, liquids, and gels getting through security or being allowed on the plane. Because I was always fearful of being separated from my trusted kit, having it get lost in luggage and being shipped to another destination or being tampered with during an inspection, it always traveled with me. An unknowing baggage handler chucking my kit onto a luggage rack, shattering my powders, would be a nightmare. Turning the kit upside down could destroy several hundred dollars' worth of makeup. I'm not sure how I would overcome the travel restrictions of today.

I received endless instructions about our itinerary. Young, bilingual American students studying in China would be our translators to help us maneuver through this foreign land.

"You'll need to pack your own snacks; you'll be on location. Don't hesitate to share your snacks and provisions with your Chinese guides. If it is mealtime, do not delay your driver or any Chinese locals; it may be just a small bowl of rice or the only meal they are getting that day." We were also told not to "over tip." How can that be? People in the service industry live on their tips, at least in America. But, yes, we were told if you have an hour and a half massage that might cost you just $10, and your inner angels would want to tip $50 or even $100, please don't do that. Better to give a small gift, such as food or treats or to tip commensurate with what you are paying.

Having this new knowledge, my luggage burgeoned with individually packaged bags of raisins, granola bars, peanut butter crackers, and all things non-perishable. On one such excursion in Beijing, I remember giving one of our Chinese guides two packages of gum as a thank you for his services that day. It had been an eight- or ten-hour day, and it hardly seemed like an appropriate gesture for a very long day. The expression on his face was that of having received a prized possession. As he repeatedly thanked me for my generosity, he told me that he was going to bring the packages of gum home to his child and multigenerational family. I will never forget the unspeakable gratitude on his face.

The day had arrived. I flew out of San Francisco. With my makeup kit tucked securely under my airline seat, we took flight. It was what seemed like an endless journey. Sitting still is not my forte. This was a huge contributing factor as to why sitting in a classroom was torture for me. As I sat—or I should say tried to sit—paced, and restlessly fidgeted through what seemed like a marathon, the flight finally came to an end. A mere twenty-seven hours later, with two connections and layovers, I had arrived at the Beijing Capital International Airport.

Going through customs was everything you would expect and hope to avoid—mind-numbing. Continuous lines of people, patiently and impatiently waiting, while uniformed guards scrutinized paperwork. Once I successfully cleared the hurdles of transpacific travel, I was greeted by a car and driver, and we headed to the hotel. I was so relieved to have had many logistics taken care of for me.

We traveled through the streets of Beijing, already showing signs of unrest. I was immediately struck by the throngs of bicycles going in every direction. Husbands were peddling the primitive machines, skillfully maneuvering the roundabouts of the city, and mothers were sitting side-saddle on the backs of the bicycles, carrying a small child. People. Lots and lots of people. There was an undercurrent of what was to come, but mostly calm. Overwhelming calm.

We arrived at the hotel and pulled up to the drive. The driver pulled my overstuffed suitcase from the trunk, despite his small, slight frame. I crossed the threshold into the lobby of the hotel and was immediately taken aback. Let's say dumbfounded. After Moscow, I did not know what to expect. I had literally stepped into another world. If I didn't know better, I would say that I was in a 5-star hotel on Madison Avenue in Manhattan. I looked in awe at the ceilings that towered above me, with pendulums of chandeliers casting a glitter over the room. Long panels of colorful fabric draped the windows. Beautifully upholstered furniture was arranged for people to gather, orchestrated on ornate oriental rugs. Artwork was displayed with an eye for detail. The gift shop was elegant, with stacks and stacks of oriental rugs, something you would see in a showroom at market. I thought to myself, *I guess this is what you might refer to as the haves and have-nots.*

We always started our day with a quick makeup call, to prepare Dan for his daily broadcast. Today was a series of the landmarks and history of the city of Beijing. As we're finishing up, Dan hands me an envelope full of cash and says, "Can you help me with some shopping? I know I won't have time to find something special."

I was caught off guard and asked for more information.

"Who am I shopping for?"

He said, "I need two gifts for my wife and my daughter, maybe jewelry."

"Okay. Tell me more about them." I learned that his wife was an artist and that he had one daughter. I counted out the money in front of him, to ensure that we both knew how much money he was entrusting me with. It was over $200, and the exchange rate was very favorable. At some point later in the trip, and after agonizing over my choices, I selected some sophisticated and understated pieces. When I later gave the gifts with the remaining money back to Dan, he was very grateful and somewhat relieved. *What a nice gesture,* I thought to myself, *to be thinking of such a thing amidst turmoil, chaos, and an erratic work schedule.*

First stop, The Forbidden City. There were too many crew members for one vehicle. Unless we were going to magically squeeze into a small clown car, someone would need to travel separately. I rode with one other tech crew and a driver, arriving at our destination before the rest of the team. Two of us piled into a small automobile and bounced along the streets of Beijing. I am again struck by the drab colors of all the people on the streets, the tourists easily distinguishable from the people of China. The residents were always moving in their calm manner, always polite and understated, in contrast with the boisterous onlookers and their cameras, draped around their necks. I was dismayed that the tourists were always traveling in groups; no one dared venture out on their own.

The square and palace were hauntingly deserted. The press had been given special privilege to enter the majestic gates. The tranquility was breathtaking—dragons, palaces, jade, and ivory in every direction you looked. We were surrounded by oceans of red and gold, with the ornate script that was so foreign to my eyes. Full-story images of Mao Tse-Tung hung high overhead. I asked my teammate to take a photo of me, hopping up onto the metal barrier of the fenced dragon. The jaded beast was massive, with ornate carvings showing every detail, down to the toenails on his paws. I mimicked the posture of the statue, a growling expression on my face. I reflect on this moment and think about my decision to take the photo in this way. A guest in a Communist country—if not extremely dangerous, then at least naïve and disrespectful to their culture and holy space. I think that perhaps the well-traveled and well-educated would have cringed; if not, I certainly would have been reprimanded.

Next stop, the Great Wall of China. Having been on many shoots by now with CBS, I became accustomed to having people stop us, to ask for an autograph or photo with Dan Rather. We would often travel in a beehive surrounding him, to try and stay on schedule and avoid these niceties. While at the Great Wall, Dan was tapped on the shoulder. There was a young couple holding a camera. He turned to greet the people and politely acquiesce—then was handed a camera. The young couple asked him if he wouldn't mind taking their photo. He was momentarily caught off guard and then openly laughed. He graciously took the camera and snapped a photo of the young couple, then handed the camera back. I found this interaction humorous and humbling at the same time and admired the way he had handled it. I snapped a photo of him taking the photo to memorialize the moment. A photo of a photo. It keeps you real.

The protest continued to build. As the scene began to deteriorate, the crowds began to sprawl, and the sanitary conditions worsened. It no longer made sense for Dan to be wearing a suit and tie. The men on the crew all donated pieces of clothing to piecemeal Dan's wardrobe so that he wouldn't look like a fish out of water. A khaki coat from someone, a sweater from someone else, and a shirt made up his ensemble. Mission accomplished. We were all family. As we worked together to film this multi-day documentary, I was also put in charge of helping coordinate Dan's wardrobe. For continuity and sequencing of the story, I had to ensure that he was wearing the same wardrobe for the appropriate shoot. I was amused by this industry. Makeup artist, personal shopper, wardrobe assistant. I found myself wearing many hats, and I enjoyed it.

I learned a lot on the trip. The simple things that Americans take for granted, the young college students of China were willing to risk their lives for. The young men and women who worked in the factories also lived in the factories. They would labor by day, entering one door by morning, then walk around to the other side of the building at night and enter another door to their cramped accommodations. Food was scarce to many—the "have-nots." I repeatedly found myself sharing my snacks with our Chinese guides and only wished that I had more to give.

Women would have their menstrual cycles graphed on a chart in the factories for all to see, to ensure that they were not hiding pregnancies. The privilege of having more than one child was not afforded to these citizens. How could they possibly confirm this data? What protocol must these women go through on a monthly basis to prove this? It was dehumanizing. I was moved to tears. Every American woman at one time has found themselves profusely embarrassed when a tampon would fall out of their purse at an inopportune time, yet these women were being sterilized after delivering a baby, against their will, to again ensure that there would not be another pregnancy. What it must have felt like to have such an invasion of privacy of the most basic human rights is beyond my understanding.

As we drove through the streets of Beijing, I watched the crude sanitary conditions of the people on the street. Toddlers would be dressed in baggy trousers, with an opening through the crotch of the pants. If they needed to use the restroom, their mother would stop what they were doing, have them squat in the street, do their business, clean them up, then get back onto their bicycles and be on their way. It was so commonplace that no one even took note.

I had wondered how adults solve this quandary. Where were the porta potties? Or I should say, *were* there porta potties? I quickly learned. Once we had begun filming, we had been on location in Tiananmen Square for several hours, and I needed to use the facilities. I asked Dan, "Where are the temporary restrooms?" He pointed across the oceans of people to a draped area. *Okay,* I thought. *This should be interesting.*

"Okay, I'll be back," I said.

"No, no. You can't go alone," he replied. "Bob, will you escort LuAnn to the restroom." This was said more as an instruction rather than a question. As we all became family on these trips, we all tried to help each other out. Bob Simon, award winning journalist—three Peabody awards, twenty-seven Emmy awards, and the President's award. Yes, that Bob Simon. I stocked my pockets with tissues from my makeup kit and smiled modestly. He graciously walked with me to the draped area. I pulled away the cloth to enter and found a trench over the sewer system. The details of what you might expect need go without further explanation. Like an expectant husband waiting at a hospital, Bob waited for me outside of the draped area, and then we made the trek back. It keeps you real.

As the days progressed, the square began to fill with more and more people. The hopeful students had staged a hunger strike, to express a peaceful protest for democracy. They had crafted an underground student paper and were distributing it to the crowds to communicate and share their message. As the days passed and the military had not yet stepped in, the students gained confidence and the protest gained momentum. Within a few days, we began to see older people on the streets; and by the final days, children began to assemble, too. I looked at the young kindergarten students in their brightly colored uniforms, a stark contrast to that of the drab and dark colors of the adults.

While history was being made in Tiananmen Square by student protesters, more history was being made on the tarmac greeting "Gorby" into China. Young college students, peaceful and calm, filled the streets. With the vast number of protesters in Tiananmen Square, the Chinese government made the decision to stage a short ceremony at the airport and forgo the planned ceremony and tour. President Gorbachev was greeted at the airport for a brief fanfare of pageantry with a uniformed military band and then swept off to his hotel. Five-star, no doubt.

On May 20, Dan was going to pull an all-nighter. He was going to walk amongst the local people, the young protesters, and get footage of this historical moment. Knowing full well that the next few days were going to be hard, and given the option to stay at the hotel, I decided that it might be best to get a good night's sleep. I prepared Dan's makeup for the night and remained back at the hotel.

The following day, I awaited the executive producer in the lobby of our hotel to join our driver and head to Tiananmen Square. He tentatively said, "He's been up all night. Do you have your bag of tricks? He's going to be a mess." I nodded politely and more accurately thought, *He's going to look like hell.*

We made the short drive and arrived at Tiananmen Square, all the while having the crowds cheering and clapping for the American cameras and press. The crowds were bigger than life. The protesters had drug large sewer pipes across roadways to block the tanks. The mob had grown to over a million people. They were everywhere—in the streets, climbing fences, on rooftops, and in the trees. My heart was pounding. I was on an adrenaline high.

We made our way to the flatbed truck. We were surrounded by people on all sides, everywhere you looked. Students were carrying signs and banners and waved to greet "the Americans." You could read the wonder on their faces. *What was all of this strange equipment?* I remember making an observation of the young students and understood their wonder. No one had cell phones, Walkman radios, or technology of any kind. I comically thought, *Isn't everything "Made in China?"*

I began to unpack my kit, and the television crew is wiring Dan to begin the live broadcast. The control room at the network back home had us under their magnifying glass. As we're getting set up, in the middle of nowhere, almost on cue, the cell phone rings. In 1989, cell phones looked more like a large, handheld walkie-talkie.

In midstream of my preparations, the producer stops me. "Don't touch him. New York says no makeup. He goes on air just like that!"

Okay. There goes my career. This will impress my clients back home, I thought sarcastically. I offered him a bottle of water and brushed the hair out of his face. It keeps you real.

Dan was standing on top of a crate, a vantage point for filming. He loved the hunt of the story. As the people surrounded the truck, I began to question our safety. If the military were to act and everyone started to run, would we be trampled? Then it began to happen.

The choppers came from out of nowhere. At first there was just one, then more and more. They looked like a swarm of giant bugs hovering above us, descending on the flatbed truck. The bodies of the eight helicopters were camouflage and dark in color, sent from the Communist Chinese Party to disperse the previously peaceful protesters. The immense blades were casting dirt and gravel, and the sound was deafening.

The television crew was on the flatbed truck—an attempt to separate us from the thousands of people in the streets. A journalist sat cross-legged on the truck, with a typewriter and makeshift desk on his lap. The Communist Party was about to declare martial law, and any communications to the rest of the world would be blocked. He furiously tapped away at the story, racing against the clock. The sound and tech crew were left to fend for themselves, gathering equipment amidst the chaos.

I watched the crowd in their drab colors begin to flee, an ocean of movement beginning to build like a tidal wave. The numbers had grown over the past few weeks to over a million, and it was more than the government was willing to tolerate.

As the scene began to escalate, Dan yelled at us, "Get to the car!" I grabbed my makeup bag, and we began to scramble toward the vehicle as if our lives depended on it. And they did. The driver and car were within view, and we somehow managed to find our way amidst the turbulent winds. "Soak your towels in water and be prepared to cover your faces! They may use chemical warfare! Get on the floor of the car."

I felt my heart begin to race. I grabbed the grey and blue towels from my makeup kit and soaked them with water from my water bottle. Looking back, I think I was so naive that I didn't know what to be afraid of. Was I really in any kind of real danger?

BBC, ABC, NBC, and CNN were all there. This was going to be groundbreaking news. What I came to learn was that the government had just proclaimed martial law. They were going to disconnect our power and pull the plug, and with it our ability to broadcast. We still had the satellite dish at the hotel, so our immediate mission was to get back to the hotel and try to get the story out. The short, thirty-minute drive from Tiananmen Square to the Beijing hotel was done in fifteen minutes. We rush into the lobby with a burst of energy, cameras, CBS identification badges, and whatnot.

As we're moving through the hotel, a crowd from the lobby begins to follow "the action." Certainly, this was more entertaining than the smoked salmon and shrimp cocktail! We're followed through the lobby by hotel guests as we race up the elevator, into a hallway, and near the control room. I was following Dan and didn't know that they were already filming. Unexpectantly, I found myself on camera. I immediately ducked into a doorway to get out of view.

As if on cue by the Keystone Cops, we quickly moved outside to the satellite dish. Dan called out to me from across a crowd of people. During the chaotic scramble from the flatbed truck, we all grabbed as much as we could, and I ended up with his bag. The helicopters at Tiananmen Square had stirred up dust clouds, and he could no longer depend on his contacts. He needed his glasses. I quickly dug through his bag to find his glasses and realized that they must have fallen out. We were by now in a grassed courtyard, and my job description just added "bloodhound." I quickly began retracing our steps in systematic rows, back and forth, to see where his glasses may have fallen out. I prayed, and miraculously I found them. The show must go on.

As we move through the hotel, there's an American guest—a short, stocky gent—trying to get a photo and autograph from Dan Rather, mid-broadcast, and crowding the shot. "I have a lot of stock in CBS," he says, as if this would matter in the midst of shit hitting the fan. I'm trying to help, to intervene and talk with this gentleman, to ask him to step back. Makeup artist, personal shopper, wardrobe assistant, bloodhound, bodyguard.

I often felt as though Dan Rather had eyes in the back of his head. He begins snapping his fingers at the crew, trying to get their attention to help me out. At some point, he turns to the fan and asks him politely if he wouldn't mind giving him some room to work.

Meanwhile, the Chinese authorities were already there, trying to stop the broadcast. Dan is doing a song and dance, a soft shoe, almost, to try and stall for time. The other crew members were trying to get images sent from the violence that was erupting in the square to New York before losing the signal, and he is playing both negotiator and reporter at the same time. Blowing smoke, to stall.

As we have now run out of time and patience runs thin on the part of the Chinese, Dan signs off to America, the screen goes to hash, and we are done. Martial law has been declared. This was the last CBS broadcast from Beijing. Dan now takes a moment to speak with the fan and allow him the opportunity to take a photo together.

If you have ever felt like the air was let out of your balloon, this was that time. With martial law being declared and unable to broadcast, we no longer had a purpose for being in China. Dan was flown out of Beijing immediately. I turned around, and he was gone. The crew needed to get packed up. We did not know how or when we would be leaving or whether flights could be changed. The summit was not going to go forward as planned. "Keep a low profile," we were told. "We have credentials and may not be stopped. They don't want the press here."

I remember looking outside of my hotel room that evening to a full moon. It was an eerie feeling, almost. Unsure of how or when we could get out of Beijing, I felt isolated, lonely, and fearful.

This is when the story starts to sound a little like the scene from *The Titanic*. The next morning, as I pass through the lobby, there's a chamber orchestra performing in the formal dining room, in their concert black tuxedos. White linen tablecloths draped the tables, and china and crystal sparkled below the chandeliers. It was a stark dichotomy. The hotel guests had no way of knowing what was transpiring across the city. Apparently, due to all the chaos on the streets, all tours had been cancelled, and the guests were not allowed to leave the hotel. The disgruntled guests at the hotel were having brunch, changing their flights to return home, yet there were no cabs, limousines, or private transportation available.

As it turns out, on May 22, 1989, I was able to fly home. The government was all too willing to have us gone. The airport was packed, but we had credentials and the clout of the network behind us. The haves and the have-nots.

A week later, life returns to normal, and I find myself in a local hair salon in Fort Worth, Texas, almost as if the past two weeks were a surreal dream. I struck up a casual conversation with the lady sitting next to me in the chair and learned that she, too, had been in Beijing the previous week. I remember feeling that same eerie feeling wash over me as she recounted her story. Karma had me in its sights.

On June 5, 1989, "Tank Man" was splashed across the American newspapers, the unknown activist blatantly standing to block the tank. On June 19, 1989, *Time* magazine unveiled its cover with the same image. Thirty years later, on the anniversary of the Tiananmen Square protests, a monument was erected in the Mojave Desert in Fang Zheng's honor. He looked on from his wheelchair where he sits, his two legs and lower body crushed from the impact of the tank.

My entire childhood we were told that we had to clean our plates. "Eat your green beans." Some poor children on the other side of the world didn't have enough to eat. As a young girl, I always thought my mom was making it up. Because we were from a large family, we were taught that food must not go to waste. Having spent just a short time in China, I truly came to appreciate the freedoms and abundance we have grown accustomed to in the United States. In 1989, I came to have a different appreciation for my blessings.

Dan Rather: American Journalist; Tiananmen Square
https://danratherjournalist.org/ground/
crises-and-conflicts/tiananmen-square/
compilation-tiananmen-square-videos/video-tiananmen-4

Tiananmen Square.

The Forbidden City.

A photo of a photo: "It keeps you real."

Bob Simon in China.

The protests begin to build.

The Haves...

...and the Have-Nots.

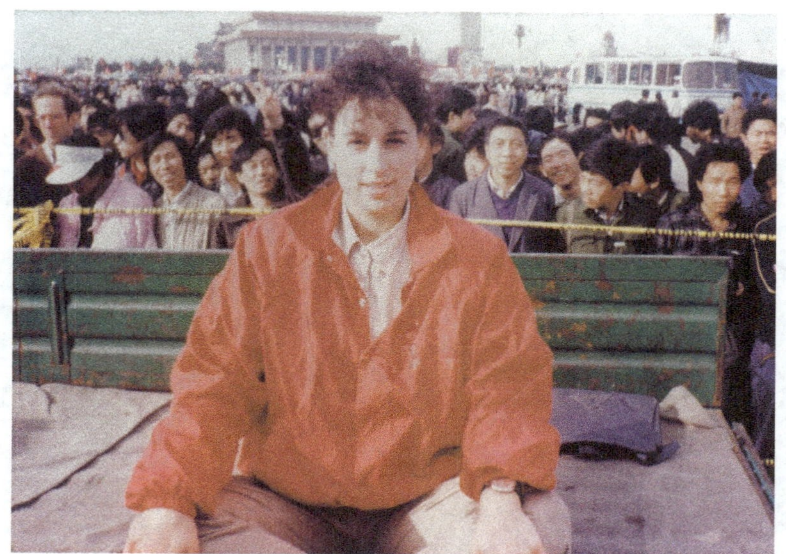

Peaceful Protesters.

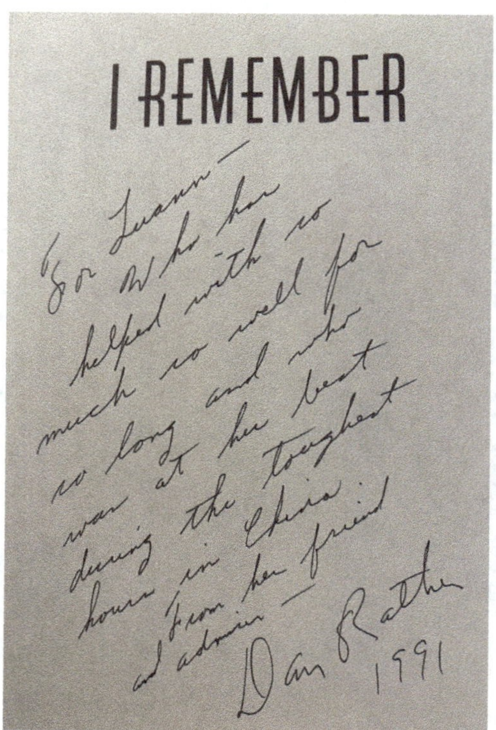

I Remember – Dan Rather

The Birthday Party - 1991
"A Seat at the Table"

It would be a six-day gig, a week-long tour, really, beginning at TCU in Fort Worth just ten minutes from my studio and concluding in Austin for the milestone birthday celebration. Many jobs over the years included excruciatingly long hours, early mornings, long travel, and hotel rooms. This week would not be one of those weeks. This was the fun part! The days were filled with live broadcasts, billboard shoots, luncheons, cocktail parties, and chartered airplanes, puddle jumping across the state. Our hosts were more than happy to roll out the red carpet for us.

Everywhere we landed was the locale of the evening broadcast. As we travelled from city to city, the camera crew would alternate, the lighting crew would rotate, but I was like gum on his shoe, always the constant in his immediate staff. We became so much like family; I looked forward to the Texas pecan pie I received every Thanksgiving.

On one such trip in a small, chartered plane, it was just the pilot, "Rather," and me. I had already placed the motion-sickness patch behind my earlobe and prepared for the flight. The overhead fan was creating a stream of air on my clammy skin, and I tried to put my mind and body into a Zen-like mindset. I feel myself beginning to sweat, I begin to fan myself, and apparently Dan notices my discomfort, as well. He begins to question me, always the journalist, asking if I'm having a panic attack. Do I have a fear of flying? As the scenario unfolds, and the small plane is circling waiting for clearance to land at D/FW, I see him leaning into the cockpit and saying in a rather firm voice to the pilot, "We've got to get this plane down." Witnessing that I'm unable to control my nausea, he reaches for a trash can and hands it to me, ensuring that I have an option, and this won't become a lasting memory. Once the plane touched down, he quickly exited the plane, faster than I've ever seen him move.

It was kind of him to give me a moment of privacy—not that anyone would want to stick around for that sensory experience. Unfortunately, I still had to maneuver through a full workday. I cleaned myself up with the wet wipes from my makeup kit and freshened myself with a water bottle and gum as I walked across the tarmac to the awaiting town car with the new broadcast team. I said to myself, *Boy, I guess I've arrived, travelling in a private chartered jet, landing in D/FW, when I have Dan Rather handing me a trash can so that I can vomit.*

The six days were filled nonstop with hurry up and wait. Our many conversations over the course of the trip included stories about my studio and the trials and tribulations of being a small business owner. We were now just a short drive from the studio. It was a mystery to the team as to why I would remain in Fort Worth, having been offered a job in New York. I desperately wanted the crew to see my years of blood, sweat, and tears—to see why I couldn't just walk away. The studio was a dream fulfilled and one of my most significant accomplishments.

"We have to eat. How about I order some sandwiches? My staff can have lunch ready, and then we can drive on to Dallas for the next gig."

After only a small bit of arm twisting, the team agreed we could make this happen. The car pulled into the quiet community on Byers Avenue, my business being one of only a few within a residential area. It was a feat I was proud of, to get the neighbors on board to grant my petition for a business permit and zoning in 1984.

"Pull up to the front to unload, and we can park the car in the back."

We pulled up to the studio, which began as a small two-bedroom home, rezoned and converted into the charm of a cottage, now reimagined into a pastel innovation of peach, pink, blue, and lavender. The colors were chosen with confidence, but it was a saga of trial and error as to which color would ornament the walls and which color would embellish the columns. The final palette was not created on the first try. Framed photographs of beauty queens, celebrities, and people of distinction lined the hallway walls.

Our team stepped through the wrought iron door into the lobby to be greeted by my staff, standing at attention. It was such a display of admiration, it felt almost like a commander inspecting her troops. They all very much wanted to meet this legend of journalism and were dressed for a party. I wondered whether I had missed my invitation! From the reception area you could see my workstation, proudly on display. The arched mirrors were framed with theatrical stage lights, which could be dimmed for different settings. The sunshine beaming in from the exterior, west-facing window provided natural light for daytime makeup.

I suggested that Dan take his thirty minutes of downtime for himself and lunch in my office before leaving for our next taping in Dallas. We would be on the road for at least another hour. Always being under the magnifying glass must be exhausting to a person in the spotlight.

The high-paced world of journalism doesn't always allow for a professional makeup artist, so I convinced Dan to let me give him a quick lesson and select some travel products for him. I made a point of videotaping the lesson, and I had a graphic designer sketch Dan's face onto a sketch pad for me, so that I could apply color to the sketch. Dan could then later refer to the sketch. I had selected an understated black vinyl travel bag for his supplies. He modestly took in the lesson, while my adoring staff tried to unsuccessfully appear indifferent. The synchronized lesson meant that he was now ready for his evening broadcast.

The trip to Fort Worth culminated with a lavish birthday celebration in Austin. CBS was orchestrating a party, with the loving guidance of Dan's wife Jean and his daughter Robin. Wayne had called me to let me know I would need cocktail attire. Typically, I wouldn't be travelling with this type of clothing. I don't know that I expected the party to be so large—what felt like over a thousand people. I received an emergency phone call for eyeliner that went AWOL for Wayne's wife, and once that mishap was resolved, it was time to celebrate. The ballroom was filled with large, round tables and chairs, all positioned towards the front of the room for the festivities. The head table was located directly in front of the stage for the guest speakers to address and recognize the guest of honor.

We were led into the room, almost like a mother duck and her ducklings, for all to see.

The small entourage made its promenade to the front of the room, to a table designated for the guests of honor; a floral centerpiece signaled its prominence. Guests of all ages looked on, hoping to get a few words with the man of the hour.

There were no place cards on the table, only the designated number of chairs. As the chairs began to fill, it became apparent that there were not enough seats at the table, an awkward moment of musical chairs, with one odd man out. Or I should say, one woman out.

The hostess gently took my elbow and led me to another table towards the back of the room. The table was partially filled, with a few remaining chairs for unnamed guests. Apparently, this was the table for misfit toys. It was at this time that I wished I hadn't dressed in a royal blue pantsuit, drawing attention like a blinking neon light. I would prefer not to think of myself as a wallflower, but right then a bland beige would have suited me just fine. I sat down at the table, determined to dust off my pride and enjoy the party. There are less honorable situations in life; I have overcome far worse than a seating arrangement.

Sixty seconds into the evening—and before I had time to even introduce myself to the others at the table—up the aisle marches A.J., a 5'1" powerhouse frame in spiked high heels, public relations liaison for the CBS affiliates.

"I'm fine, really. It's not a big deal."

"No, no, no. We've made room at the table. You'll be joining us. LuAnn doesn't sit in the back of the room."

And in a procession back to the front of the hall, royal blue pantsuit and all, we make our way back to the floral centerpiece. Nothing to see here. My friends and colleagues were scooting closer together so that one more place setting could be added to the table.

I don't remember much about the meal, or the rest of the evening, for that matter, just how I felt—honored to hold a seat at the table, among family. It was comforting. Rewarding. I was with my tribe.

"Okay. Let's go!" he said, willing to stretch the boundaries and step outside of his comfort zone.

It was many years later that I first introduced the airbrush to Dan. He was reluctant to make changes of any kind. He liked the consistency, as did the network. As we hopped, skipped, and jumped through the cities of Texas, each day landing in a different city, the CBS affiliates rolled out the red carpet with luncheons and cocktail parties. The PR department, management, and local anchormen and anchorwomen lined up to greet us. Dan was doing the afternoon radio broadcast and the local news, followed by the national evening news. I had been airbrushing for a few months, confident enough to introduce it to him. I knew it would be a challenge to convince him to consider something new.

"This is a good place to test the waters."

"No, no, no. You know how the network is. New York likes me to look consistent."

"Just listen for a minute. Everything has gone high definition. I want to try something new. If you don't like it, you have nothing to lose." He had to really think about it.

Once I had him on board, I was excited, and honored, really, that he was willing to let me make changes. If he looked good, I looked good. I custom blended the foundation on the spot for his skin tone to get a perfect match. I explained to him that he would like it better because it requires less makeup. He looked at himself in the mirror, did the local broadcast, and I packed away the airbrush.

As we gathered for the evening news, I lined up my old school tools of the trade from the beginning of time. Thinking that the airbrush had already had its debut, I proceeded with the status quo. We would talk about the airbrush down the road; he was not going to risk it for the national news. He sat down in the makeup chair, I caped him, and he began looking around, as if he had misplaced his reading glasses.

"What are you looking for?"

"Where's your little airbrush machine?"

"Oh, you liked it?" I replied, smiling.

"I did."

"Okay. Let's do it."

New York didn't catch the change to his makeup the first time, and there was no complaint for the remainder of the week. Our next trip concluded in Seattle, with the Los Angeles crew and equipment. We were on an outdoor shot, the lighting had been converted to HD, and the lighting director was complimenting the makeup.

"I don't know what you did, but it's perfect for high definition."

"Let's see what New York says."

We didn't have to wait long; we heard from the network that same day. "New York likes it." The airbrush had made its debut with the CBS News Division.

On location in Seattle with "48 Hours."

Wendell Abbott - 1991

"Surrogate Father"

It was a lazy day on the lake. The sun was high in the sky, and the water was calm. The ripples of water formed concentric circles as it bounced off the sides of the small motorboat. Wendell and I floated aimlessly, with no regard for time. It was a well-earned day off, and we were going to make the most of it.

We were solving the problems of the world, talking endlessly about the events of the day and the minutiae that consumed our worlds. One topic that kept rising to the surface like a returning tide was my age. More specifically, my unfaltering desire to have a child. I was thirty-five. The clock was ticking. I had gone through a divorce many years prior, like most of my friends. Wendell, too, had been in a marriage for fifteen years, the union ending in divorce.

We talked about the years slipping away. If I were to predict where my life would be now, it would not be this. I had been divorced for many years. I was not remarried, I was not in a relationship, and there was no one on the horizon. I was chasing my career, and it was stable. I was travelling, but nothing that couldn't be overcome. I had the means to provide a secure and loving home for a child.

More importantly, out of the blue, CBS had offered me a position in New York. I questioned my life, wondering whether to sell my business and relocate. I considered whether to try to operate my business in Fort Worth with a partner or manager, while residing in New York.

I wanted to go to New York. It would be a feather in my cap. But I also knew deep in my heart that if I went to New York, I most likely would never marry again, and there would be no one to call me Mom.

The small motorboat continued to drift along the banks of the lake, amidst the green algae and the brown water that was churned up from the shallow waters below. Wendell looked at me and spoke casually, almost as if he were asking me to pick up a gallon of milk from the grocery store.

"I have an idea. We can have a baby."

"Oh, really?" I replied, with a look of apprehension and my mouth forming what resembled a smirk.

"Yeah. We could have a baby. You go take that job in New York. I can fly back and forth with the baby. We can go back and forth."

Wendell and I had never had a sexual relationship. We had never had any sexual tension or attraction to each other. We had never even kissed. I knew that he had been married before, but any sexual relationship he may have had after that time was kept private.

I did not respond immediately, trying to read his expression. I folded my arms across my chest and said, "Well…we'd have to have artificial insemination."

This was when Wendell looked at me with one of his cat-that-ate-the-canary grins. He paused and looked directly into my eyes. "You'd be surprised."

We talked, considering the concept. I pondered over my life and my future. I was overwhelmed by his offer and deeply touched. For someone to make such a proposal was moving. But to then consider taking on the role of parent for the unforeseeable future demonstrated his love for me.

I thought about it for a fleeting moment. With our eyes fully open, we both concluded that having two parents in two different states, being carted back and forth, would be a horrible life for a child. We put the idea to rest, never speaking about it again.

Wendell was a giver. He would have been a good father. He would live in the moment and live life to the fullest. When God comes to call, he will be ready.

Wendell, he would have been a good father.

Oklahoma City Bombing,
One-Year Memorial - April 1996

"Seven Seconds"

I love a good romantic comedy film. I love the idea of being in love. Relationship failures didn't keep me from trying again, which is how I often found myself in relationships doomed to failure. Trying to put Humpty Dumpty back together again. I had to take a risk and have an open heart. Searching for a fairytale relationship included a blissful ending of having a child. After another attempt at the traditional path of love and marriage, and although the marriage did not survive, at the age of thirty-eight I was blessed with Shannon in October of 1994. If I had not taken the chance at love, I would not have had my daughter.

It was Mother's Day of 2021 when I sat down to put pen to paper to begin this story. Shannon had phoned first thing to wish me a happy Mother's Day. We would meet later in the evening for dinner. On April 19 of 1995, Timothy McVeigh would commit mass murder. His weapon of choice, a rented Ryder truck filled with explosives. It was heartbreaking to think that while I pondered the chicken Thai salad or the beef pepper steak, the families of the Oklahoma City bombing of the Alfred P. Murrah Federal Building mourned the loss of their children on Mother's Day, their mother, or their loved ones. They would not be having a meal to celebrate and show gratitude to mothers. Families of 168 victims and hundreds of survivors only calculated how many years they have spent this holiday alone.

We were on American soil, at the site of the Oklahoma City bombing, in the heart of downtown. An American terrorist attack on American soil. The grass lay dormant in April of 1996, now one year since the bombing. Most of the devastation had been cleared away. The area was surrounded by a six-foot construction fence, although construction on the memorial was not scheduled to begin for another year. President Bill Clinton and First Lady Hillary Clinton were on the grounds two weeks prior to lay a wreath, with its floral array of color and streamers of lavender and blue. In the distance, the lonely shell of a building stood, the panes of glass now absent from their window frames. A steady flow of traffic signaled that for some, life was moving on.

We were working outdoors, and it became evident that makeup would not be needed. There would be no need for glamour. I had been hired by CBS to prepare Dan Rather for the evening news and any "guests" who wished to have makeup. The guests would include families of victims. "Guests" was a shallow description for this occasion.

I introduced myself, not knowing who I would meet. Typically, I chat, it is light-hearted, and we learn something about each other. In this case, I introduced myself and added, "I'm sorry for your loss."

She was a mother of two. She had no living children. She was brave, prepared to tell her story. Again. Tears began to roll down my face, at first slowly, then uncontrollably. I tried to find words, but instead I found myself weeping, unable to control my tears. I began to pray, asking for strength to finish my work. *Please give me strength. Please diminish her pain.* I was mute, unable to speak.

She was polite and appreciated my empathy for her loss—almost stoic, numbed by events of the last year. She was understandably still very raw. I felt my eyes swelling with tears and could not see past my magnifying glasses to apply makeup. I tried to freshen her hair and makeup before going on camera, but really it was me unable to function. She and I embraced.

"Please know that I will be praying for you."

The daycare was in the corner of the building. It was her birthday. Her mother worked in the same building. She considered not going into work that morning but would only stay for a bit. She left her two young boys at daycare for the last time.

When the building shook, she was about to have birthday cake. Seeing the pile of rubble where the daycare once stood, she knew. She spoke of shock, anger, unbearable grief, forgiveness, and finally renewal. Someday she hoped to have another child.

There were no words to express the pain that was transferred to me that day, the best that I could imagine not having lived through it. I felt as though I were on an emotional roller coaster. It had been a long, four-hour drive from Fort Worth. I wasn't sure what I would be walking into. It was a restless night of sleep, waking every thirty minutes. It felt like two days of "attending a funeral." Above all, I felt guilt for being thankful that it wasn't me, having a two-year-old and a mother who was still living.

I wanted to get home. I needed to get home. I entered my daughter's bedroom that evening to a darkened room. She was already asleep, surrounded by "dolly," her pillow, and her favorite blanket. The rail was secured on her oak daybed, which was trimmed in layers of ruffles and floral print.

I leaned in close to kiss her on the forehead, smelling her familiar scent, and felt her warmth against my skin. A loss of any kind can make you recognize how fast you can lose someone. A tragic loss makes you hold on even tighter. I was so sad for the loss of the victims; the parents, husbands, and wives, but so much worse for people who had lost children.

It was evenings like this that brought depth and maturity to my life. The nature of the industry lends itself to glamour—an illusion. If my career had taken me down a different path, only to be surrounded by beauty, I would have burned out after twenty years. Now, finding myself within the news industry with skilled journalists chasing news stories, it was a not-so-subtle wake-up call.

The northern structure of the building took just seven seconds to collapse. It is a dark reminder of how quickly life can change. Life is not yours to keep forever, but to cherish.

The Oklahoma City National Memorial was completed in February of 2001.

"We come here to remember those who were killed, those who survived and those changed forever. May all who leave here know the impact of violence. May this memorial offer comfort, strength, peace, hope and serenity." Oklahoma City National Memorial Museum

John Grisham

"A Time to Kill"

In 1989, John Grisham wrote his first novel, which became an instant best seller. The book was banned in Texas public schools because of racially and sexually graphic material. The award-winning movie followed in 1996, with a blockbuster list of actors including Matthew McConaughey, Sandra Bullock, Samuel L. Jackson, Ashley Judd, Kiefer Sutherland, Donald Sutherland, Kevin Spacey, and many more. For this, being my maiden voyage onto a movie set, it was a privilege to be surrounded by an A-list cast!

While I had the opportunity to do the makeup for John Grisham's interview, there was nothing remarkable about the encounter, other than I remember thinking he looked like he'd just stepped off the golf course, after he had completed his workout at the health club. He was a very handsome man—lean, tanned, and refined. He looked like he was straight out of central casting.

What was remarkable about the day was that the film crew was going to shoot a very challenging scene. A cast of hundreds were called to the set in Canton, Mississippi, where the historic courthouse sits in the middle of the town square. The statuesque columns frame the doors of the Greek Revival structure, with its set of colonial blue paneled doors. The octagonal dome and crowning piece is placed squarely on top of the two-story building. It was apparent why the idyllic charm of the town captured the eye of the directors.

The scene involved a stunt man being set on fire and falling from the top of the structure to the ground. His costume was that of the Grand Dragon of the Klu Klux Klan of Mississippi, with its cardinal red sleeves trimmed in royal blue stripes. Underneath the costume was a fire-retardant suit. The risk of injury to the actor was great, but more specifically, the fumes from the burning suit could damage, perhaps irreparably, his lungs. The timing had to be precise. The goal was for him to hold his breath throughout this stunt, up until the time the burning suit was extinguished and could be ripped from his body. The cost for the stuntman was $100,000 each time he performed the fall. The objective on everyone's part was to do this stunt just one time.

I watched for what felt like a limitless period while the crew meticulously set the pieces in place with engineering precision. There were multitudes of mattresses and padding put in place for his fall. There was a team of firemen ready and on alert to put out the fire upon his landing. The fire department was also on hand. Cameras were placed from every angle—on tops of buildings, on the ground, and from overhead. There was so much adrenaline it was hard to know what was real and what was not.

The setup took all day. I stood shoulder-to-shoulder amongst the crowds of people watching and waiting. I was surrounded by the many actors dressed as the KKK. Sandra Bullock was standing to my right, her beauty as striking in person as on the big screen. Buses and cars filled with actors lined the streets. The intensity of the scene was unmistakable as preparations were put into place. I prayed silently to myself, *Surely I'm not going to watch somebody die today.*

The scene was shot just one time. As we watched the stuntman perform a freefall, thrashing and flailing in flames, I was holding my breath in suspense. We waited in anticipation for the team to pull off his gear. I have never seen a team move so quickly. We all breathed a sigh of relief once the scene was over. To my knowledge, no one was injured in the filming of this scene.

I anxiously waited for the film to open at the box office. I was not let down by the movie, nor were the American audiences. A two-and-a-half-hour thriller and drama, with racial tension and an emotional tug and pull attraction between leading lady Sandra Bullock and leading man Mathew McConaughey did not disappoint. But once the scene hit the cutting room floor, it changed a bit. There was no footage of the actor falling off the building, only the writhing of a body set aflame. The screaming dubbed into the audio of the film could be heard, while we all knew full well that the actor was holding his breath. Most surprisingly, the all-day shoot involving hundreds of actors, technicians, directors, and producers became thirty-three seconds of thrill on the golden screen, at the cost of $100,000, and was spliced with other footage to lengthen the segment.

A Time to Kill was written in 1989 as John Grisham's portrayal of the racial tension in the '80s. This is a reprehensible part of history that I naively thought was rounding the corner and coming to a close in America. Little did I know that the fiction of this novel was only a precursor to what would unfold in Jasper, Texas, a full decade later.

John William King – Jasper, Texas 1999

"The Lynching of James Byrd Jr. - June 7, 1998"

Jasper, Texas is a small town in the southeast corner of the state and bordering Louisiana. I had never been to Jasper before. I felt like I was driving through Mayberry, USA; it felt like 1960. The town of Jasper, just over 7,000 residents, was moving at a slower pace. There were no strangers living in town. Everyone knew everyone.

The Jasper County Courthouse is a two-story building, its simplicity placed quietly in the middle of the city square. A white clock tower sits squarely over the main entrance to add an element of grandeur to the structure. A short flight of steps leads to the paneled door. Only a few sidewalks divide the green carpet of grass surrounding the courthouse into plots.

Dan is prepped and on the move, getting footage for the broadcast. I stood with some members of the crew, awaiting the sentence outside of the courthouse.

It was a grueling trial. Jury selection, alone, took three weeks. The trial had concluded. To the relief of close friends and many loved ones, it was finally coming to an end. The first trial of three had led to a conviction of capital murder. The two remaining trials were yet to come. This was the morning that the judge would sentence the defendant, John William King, to death by lethal injection.

As I am standing outside of the courthouse, I look around. I am not alone. But to my incredulity, there are many others, some dressed in dark colors, some in white hoods. In addition to the protesters and the media circus, the Black Panthers and the Klu Klux Klan were present. The energy of the crowd was at an all-time high.

John William "Bill" King exits the courthouse, officials on either side of him. The men struggle to make their way to the van waiting to take him to Huntsville Prison. Having already undergone a trial, conviction, and now a sentence, he no longer dons a clean-cut look, suit and tie. He is now wearing the orange uniform of the prison, a bullet-proof vest, and both shackles and handcuffs. His bare forearms expose his tattoos.

Before stepping into the van, the press is shouting questions at him. "Do you have anything to say to the Byrd family?" With arrogance and no remorse in his voice, he shouts, "They can suck my dick."

I had never experienced something or someone so evil. It felt like a hollowed-out shell of humanity, with no soul.

Shawn Berry - Jasper, Texas 1999

"60 Minutes II - Behind Prison Walls"

It was evil. He was evil. I did not want to touch his skin, nor did I want his skin to touch mine. I had made the conscious decision that after the interview I would throw away any sponges that had made contact, anything that I had used on him, not to be used on any other person.

It is a fall September day, 1999, just a few short months from my first trip to Jasper. Normally this would have been a very beautiful day in Texas, the relentless heat beginning to wind down. CBS was back to film a *60 Minutes II* episode, to follow the ongoing trials.

The backroads of Jasper were covered in lush greenery, with the sounds of nature around us. We rode in a car together—the producer, the cameraman, Dan, and me. Normally I looked forward to these live tapings. Today would not be one of those times. I was anxious.

Jasper was just a four-hour drive southeast of Fort Worth. The lynching that had occurred one year prior was splattered all over the newspapers and captivated the nation. Because I had been in Jasper at the time of the trial with John William King just a few months ago, one of two other men involved in the murder, I knew a lot about the case. It was a graphic and descriptive story, and at that time I left feeling emotionally drained and saddened. I was very hesitant to sit in the room for this taping and wasn't sure that I would.

After I had completed Dan's makeup, the interview would begin with Shawn Berry's longtime girlfriend. This was a spontaneous journalism moment and was not part of the planned itinerary. She was sitting uneasily outside of the jail, on a park bench. She was a young woman of few words, pretty, but simple, wearing a blue plaid shirt. Her wavy auburn hair was pulled up off her shoulders, and she had multiple piercings in her ears. Shawn Berry was the father of her young son. Already in her own makeup, I made just a few touch-ups to her face.

The interview was brief, but I was struck by her answers. She was hopeful, perhaps naive, and I felt that she truly believed that he would receive only a few years of prison time, if that. He was simply in the wrong place at the wrong time. He was a hometown boy, living with his grandmother, and he worked at the local cinema. Shawn was just twenty-three years old at the time of the lynching, and they had their whole lives in front of them, the parents of a small toddler. The other two men involved in the case had already been convicted, had received the death penalty, and were waiting on death row.

After the interview with the mother of Shawn Berry's child, I was anxious and baffled. She spoke about him in such a different light, with sincerity and devotion.

The time had come to touch-up Shawn Berry. I was nervous, and my hands were clammy. I would use just a few sponges and a brush and never let my skin touch his. Oftentimes I will use my hands to blend powder or wipe away a smudge. I was not going to let that happen on this occasion.

When I am preparing other clients for big events, I draw energy and excitement from the room. I also try to transfer a calming energy to them. For this reason, I did not want his energy, his heinous spirit. Only a monster could be this evil.

The room was small. His attorney was close at hand. Shawn was in bright orange prison garb. A plain white T-shirt could be seen from underneath the uniform. On his feet, he wore neutral canvas tennis shoes, and he crossed and uncrossed his legs uneasily during the interview. In stark contrast, Dan Rather was dressed in full jacket and slacks, striped tie, white starched shirt, and patent leather shoes, the black polish reflecting off the camera lighting.

Two black plastic chairs were placed in the cell, facing each other. Dan Rather was seated in one chair; Shawn Berry took his place in the other, their knees almost touching. It was uncomfortably close. At the time I wondered whether this was a deliberate decision, to station the chairs so close in proximity. Was this an effort to make someone feel at ease, as though it were not an interrogation, merely a conversation between two people? Or was this merely the rules of the prison?

As he entered the room and sat down, he looked like a scared rabbit in the corner. He appeared even younger than his now twenty-four years of age, clean cut, the shadow of his facial hair barely visible. At that moment I wanted to stay for the interview.

The cameraman was directly in front of the two of them, poised and ready to begin filming, within an arm's length and just a few feet away. The space was confining. I sat cross-legged on the floor, directly below the lens of the camera, and I could feel the cold concrete through my clothing. As I listened and watched from this bird's-eye view, I almost felt like I was in a cinema, being taken down the dirt path in Jasper.

He begins to speak. June 7, 1988 was a typical summer night in Jasper. Russell Brewer was thirty-one. John "Bill" King and Shawn Berry were both twenty-three years old. They were going "woodsing." According to the Urban Dictionary, "It's kind of like hiking, but you only hike for maybe five minutes and then proceed to get drunk and high." They were all in Shawn's truck; he was the driver and the one "with the wheels."

As they made their way through the woods, a black man was hitchhiking and walking along the path ahead of them. Everyone knew who this was; he didn't need an introduction. James Byrd, Jr. was known to many in the area. He was forty-nine years old and the father of three children. The truck pulled up alongside Mr. Byrd, and he was asked whether he would like a ride.

Mr. Byrd asked where they were going. "No place in particular, just woodsing."

Mr. Byrd got into the bed of the truck, and the other two were in the front cab.

The gruesome story continues to unfold. I watch the interview as Shawn Berry finds himself unable to speak at times, fidgeting in his chair, and visibly emotional. There is a quiver in his voice. At times he is unable to make eye contact, ashamed of the details he is sharing.

All three white men had spent some time in the correction system, says Shawn. Bill and Shawn for a lesser crime of stealing cigarettes. Russell was in prison for a lengthier period and just recently released.

Shawn continues to tell his story. I'm sure he has replayed it a thousand times in his mind. By this time, the three men had exchanged places, Mr. Byrd now in the passenger seat. The truck turns down a secluded road familiar to Shawn, an area where he had grown up. As they came to a stop further into the woods, Bill and Russell hopped out of the truck bed and tried to open the passenger door of the truck where Mr. Byrd was sitting. Sensing trouble, Mr. Byrd was hanging onto the door from the inside and trying to resist the other two men. Shawn watched as the struggle ensued. At this point, Bill is quoted as saying, "F*** it. Let's kill this N*****."

According to Shawn, in a moment of reason, Shawn gets out of the truck and comes around to the passenger side of the truck to try to intervene. He tries to stop the inevitable but is quickly intimidated and backs off. "Back off, the same thing can happen to a N***** lover," he is told. As he is retelling the story, I wanted to believe him, that he was not a party to the lynching. What would I have done in his shoes? What could I have done to change the outcome?

Shawn Berry continues. The two men, Bill and Russell, grabbed Mr. Byrd and wrestled with him to the back of the truck, behind the truck on the dirt path. There had been a lot of alcohol involved. Emotions were running high, and Mr. Byrd was outnumbered by the two men. He was not a formidable match and was pushed to the ground and on all fours while the two men began to kick him, both in the ribs and in the head.

At this moment in the interview, Shawn Berry chokes up, fully understanding the humiliation that Mr. Byrd is about to endure. Russell then grabs a can of spray paint from the back of the truck bed and sprays Mr. Byrd in the face, then kicks him in the head one last time.

Mr. Byrd is no longer moving. Shawn is so petrified and overcome with fear that he is unable to move, and he urinates on himself.

Shawn Berry then goes to the front of the truck and sits in the doorjamb. He hears Russell get a chain from the back of the truck, fearful of what that could mean. He was not in view of the horrific events about to happen. Shawn is told to get in the truck, to slide in, the other two men on either side of him.

The truck drives down the dirt path with Mr. Byrd chained to the back, brutally dragging his body down the road. After a time, the men realize that the body has become detached from the truck. They back up the truck and over the dead man's body, then pull forward again to reattach the body. The lynching continues, Mr. Byrd's body bouncing along the now paved road behind the truck. The truck swings around a curve in the road and over a culvert. We later learn in forensics evidence that Mr. Byrd's head was most likely decapitated from his body at this time.

Shawn Berry goes on to state that he was so petrified he couldn't move. He had never witnessed such a violent act. Dan Rather questions, why didn't he stop them, fight them, intervene, or run? Why didn't he go to the police?

"I was scared to death. I mean, you know, it's different seeing all your heroes and stuff that you grew up watching on TV. You know, thinking if I was there, I'd done the same thing. I'd be standing right beside him, helping him, take care of all the villains and all this. But when you're there, it's a completely different story. I've never saw anything like that in my life."

Shawn describes events following the murder, that he washed the truck the following day. Dan Rather presses a little further. If he could go back in time, would he have done anything differently?

In his heavy Texan drawl, Shawn Berry goes on to say that he wished he had punched the gas, leaving the two men behind them, with Mr. Byrd safely inside the truck. The interview concludes with Shawn Berry in tears, expressing cowardice, remorse, and regret. His lawyer, Lum Hawthorne, made no objections and remained silent for the entirety of the two-hour interview.

On the trip back to our hotel, the car was quiet. There was not much conversation. We were all numb. I found myself questioning how a young person such as this could find themselves in this situation; how a life such as Mr. Byrd or Shawn Berry could change in an instant.

A mountain of evidence quickly led the police to the three men and their arrests, trials, and convictions. The Jasper jury found Shawn Berry guilty of murder, and he received a life sentence. He will be up for parole in the year 2038, at the age of sixty-four.

---

60 *Minutes II* - "Killing Time," Dan Rather, Sept 28, 1999
https://danratherjournalist.org/investigative-journalist/60-minutes-ii/killing-time/video-killing-time

New Orleans, Louisiana - September 1998

"Hurricane Georges - The Eye of the Storm"

We made our way through the French Quarter, driving through a city that was normally filled with celebration. Sometimes the streets are filled with families, standing in interminable lines to finally experience the long-awaited beignet at Cafe du Monde. Sometimes crowds are staggering along the storefronts from an excess of too much celebration. Today, the streets were eerily quiet. The French Quarter had been evacuated. There were no cars on the streets, only pools of water interrupted by our vehicle and the stillness of the overcast, dreary, and rainy day.

We were amidst the eye of the storm, with no signs of life. It was a naked city.

My initial visit to New Orleans had been with CBS, a promotional trip to meet with an affiliate. We happily embraced the charm of the bed and breakfast, filled with antiques, tapestries, ornate oriental rugs, and a proprietor that called you by your first name. This trip was exceedingly different.

It was hurricane season in New Orleans, and Hurricane Georges was expected to be a big one. We were storm chasers. Or at least most of us were. I was overtly unprepared for the conditions, my tennis shoes now soggy. I had packed my suitcase, naively unaware of how to do so for a natural disaster, kissing my now four-year-old daughter goodbye for a few days.

I walked into the hotel to be greeted by towels and sheets thrown down onto the carpet, drenched in four inches of water that had evaded the sandbags. I squished along and found my way to the second floor of the hotel, which had remained unaffected by the pooling water on the lower level of the structure.

Once I found "the team," the command post I jokingly refer to as Ground Zero was beginning to take shape. Two or three crews were huddled around the television and computer screens, engrossed as if they were in a video arcade. They were planning their strategy for filming footage. Among them was "Rather." Georges had not yet hit land. It was predicted to be a Category 4, possibly Category 5 storm.

The men were all crowded around the screens, evaluating the latest weather updates. They were all excited about catching the storm and hopeful that it was going to hit land when we were there. They loved the chase, but more so, the thrill of getting the story. As I greeted the group of six or seven men with a big smile, I said, "Y'all, there's something really wrong with you, hoping it hits where we are. I mean, you're nutburgers!" I had long discarded my facade and felt free to be myself. They laughed heartily in response, knowing full well that my assessment was accurate.

Knowing that we were soon headed to film "on location," I took the opportunity to put Rather's makeup on him before we left for the day. It was at this time that I first noticed the monogram on his sleeve, a reminder of his earlier days chasing storms. He was "the storm guy." As I'm applying the final touches onto his face, I think to myself, *This whole town is running away from this storm, and we're running smack into it. That takes some kind of mojo.*

After perusing maps, monitors, TV screens, and data, they negotiated who would ride in which truck or which car. I ended up in the short parade of vehicles, following a truck with a satellite dish attached to the roof. If we found the need to film on the spot, if we needed to power up, we had the technology to do so. It was that cool! Plastic tarps and raingear were put in place over the valuable equipment, and somewhere along the way someone loaned me a slicker and some galoshes.

We were in constant contact with New York. The planned strategy was to head north, towards Mississippi. By this time the sun is beginning to set, and nightfall is approaching.

As the storm began to bounce around the coast, we began to bounce along the two-lane road, which seemed more like swamp lands. The darkness of the night enveloped our car, with only the high beams from the headlights cutting through the dark. Water bordered either side of the road, resembling a moat. I questioned our sanity, learning about the alligators in the shallow waters and watching for live wires from downed telephone posts. These men, these storm chasers, were unphased by the challenging circumstances. Our experienced driver maneuvered skillfully, which leaves me in the relieved position to tell you about the story today.

After four or five hours of chasing Georges, the team is beginning to wither. The evacuation had left all eating establishments shut down. One crew member spoke up, almost heroically, and said, "I have food. I have stuff to eat!" Thank God.

The caravan pulled over, and he ceremoniously opened the trunk of his car to retrieve his supplies: granola bars, bottles of water, and packages of snacks. Once again, I thought, *Okay, if we get stuck, we better start rationing.* I boastfully thought to myself that had I known, I could have done better. I then reminded myself that I was the one with the soggy tennis shoes, unprepared for what was upon us.

Our journey continued through the remote landscape, chasing the elusive Georges. You could see a lone light in the distance, a beacon of hope, which turned out to be a church. Although the church had begun to flood, they had a generator on hand and offered a safe refuge. There were four or five people inside, a minister and his family. They had no intention of evacuating. They, too, were unphased by the storm. Instead, they were a harbor of hope for travelers. We all used the facilities, and the journey continued.

We encountered signage ripped by Mother Nature from buildings and strewn across the roadways. Trees were uprooted and discarded onto the ground, like unwanted toys. We confirmed that we were trailing the mystique of the storm. We had finally arrived at a chain hotel, reminiscent of the soggy carpet and pooling water back in the French Quarter. They were without electricity, but to our great relief cold sandwiches were being served from the kitchen, and we were more than appreciative.

Our adventure continued, but at some point, someone pulled the plug and the chase was abandoned. Hurricane Georges had taken a turn and hit landfall in Pascagoula, Mississippi; downgraded to a mere Category 2. There was no story. Slickers, rain boots, wet hair, and drenched clothing; there was not much need for makeup. We had filmed a quick introduction before leaving for the morning, but our mission was over. The party was over.

Upon our return to the hotel, we found that the first floor was now operational. The kitchen was fully staffed, once again a hustle and bustle. Louisianans are resilient. We met as a team for dinner and drinks, to reminisce, the "boys" saddened, as if their playdate had been cancelled. I marveled at the devotion of the television crew, bordering on addiction, to what they did, with such disregard for their own safety. It was nice to be a part of that. Once.

The following morning, I sat alone in my thoughts in the hotel restaurant, being served bacon and eggs. Any hint of the storm was already in the rear-view mirror and businesses were fully functioning. Dan Rather, his team, and the storm chasers were long gone, on to their next story, and I was headed to the airport, to my home in Fort Worth and to my daughter's four-year-old world of finger painting and macaroni and cheese. *What a weird life I have.* As weird as it was, I knew these were special times. I felt blessed.

Back home, I looked at my appointment book, thankful to control my own destiny, to embrace the structure and routine of my life. The CBS team was disheartened that the storm did not evolve into a bigger story. I was relieved. I had another story to tell. I felt like a cat with nine lives, happy to be basking in the sun.

Mikhail Gorbachev - October 1998

"Twist of Fate"

It was ironic, almost a twist of fate, that I was introducing my-self to Mikhail Gorbachev in Dallas, Texas. I had traveled to his homeland of Moscow twice, and I had been at Tiananmen Square in Beijing in 1989 for his proposed summit. Now, I find myself meeting him an hour's drive from my home in Fort Worth.

It was a last-minute decision; a late afternoon call the previous day that brought me to the State Fair of Texas. He made an appearance earlier that morning at Southern Methodist University. His day followed with a short interview with a CBS affiliate, one of the local broadcasters, and they needed me to do his makeup.

He was with his translator, although I strongly suspected that he didn't need one. I stepped into the small room with "Gorby" and his translator, expecting a cold facade of a man, a staunch Russian not meeting my gaze. I was wrong. He had a kindness in his eyes—that of someone's grandfather. He was a teddy bear. He was now sixty-seven years old and was aging well. I pulled out my airbrush, still in its infancy and new to the industry, to begin his makeup. I asked his translator to tell him that the airbrush had not yet hit the makeup world, but it would be commonplace before long. I briefly glanced at what I call his "poured wine stain" birthmark. Gorby met my gaze and spoke a few words in Russian to his translator, syllables that were unrecognizable to me. His translator turned to me and said not to cover the birthmark. It was his trademark. Quite frankly, I think he wore it like a badge of honor, distinguishable from all other foreign leaders. I later came to learn that he had won the Nobel Peace Prize in 1990, another stark difference from that of some of his colleagues. As I put the finishing touches on his face, he wrinkled his nose as the light mist hit his skin.

The interview was brief. It concluded with his host giving him a symbol of Texas as a gesture of welcome, a cowboy hat. I handed him some facial wipes to remove the makeup once the obligatory interview was complete, and he nodded with a smile. "Спасибо." We then took what I again refer to as the class picture, a photo of the group, followed by a shot with just the two of us. I packed up my kit and prepared to load my Rav4. He had more pressing things to do; he wanted to try a corndog from the Texas State Fair.

Mikhail Gorbachev – State Fair of Texas 1998

Dallas Cowboy Cheerleaders - Summer 1994

"Swimsuit Calendar - Cancun, Mexico"

It was difficult not to become desensitized to the beauty that surrounded us; the awe of the stunning landscape, the ocean and magnificent beaches, and the flawless bodies that spent hours upon hours in rehearsals and workouts, gyms and clubs. The young women ranged in age from eighteen, still in high school and waiting to graduate, to some having already started a family and well into their thirties. The provocative nature of the swimsuits and the iconic uniforms of the Dallas Cowboy Cheerleaders stopped traffic. Literally. A large gathering of twenty striking women would catch most people's eye.

As I watched crowds freeze in midstream, whisper and point, and take out cameras for a fleeting snapshot, the most pronounced event was when they were all in uniform, heading on foot to a photo shoot. The crisp white costumes customized to every curve of their bodies did not go unnoticed. The sparkling emblems of blue and silver sequined stars and oversized pom-poms shimmering in the Cancun sun stopped traffic on the interstate highways. Cars, trucks, and vans pulled over in the middle of heavy commuter traffic to stop and gape. The cheerleaders were a brilliant marketing tool for the Dallas Cowboys.

It is also difficult not to become intimidated or overwhelmed by their beauty, which most women struggle with to some degree, or to believe that this is the standard of beauty. This made the trip particularly curious, in that I was six months pregnant. But let me back up.

This was the twenty-third season for the squad. I had been contacted by the Dallas Cowboys organization to interview and watch some dance rehearsals with all forty cheerleaders. I was invited to be at the fitting of the uniforms. More importantly, they wanted to meet with me, see my portfolio, and see how I interacted with "the girls." Would I be a good fit for this highly publicized event and largely profitable project of helping to create the 1994 swimsuit calendar?

I drove to Dallas for the meet and greet, now in the early weeks of my first trimester. I had made the conscious decision not to disclose this information. Yet. In my mind, at least, I was not "showing." Once I had secured the job, it obviously needed to be discussed. I would share that fact and see whether the offer was still on the table.

After two or three interviews, more than three months later, I was made an offer to take the eight- to ten-day trip to Cancun with the entourage. My price was above the industry standard, so after some negotiation, we bartered and came up with an agreement. My salary would be 50 percent in monetary payment, and 50 percent in tickets to Dallas Cowboy football games, a coveted transaction considering there was a waitlist for tickets. Needless to say, my husband was more than thrilled with this arrangement.

During the course of the interviews, we discussed some of the details of the trip. They would be bringing twenty of their "most photogenic" girls, yet not all would be featured in the calendar. The shoot was to include all of the young women on the trip, and the final selections for the calendar would be made from the pool of photographs taken in Cancun. The team would include two hair stylists, two photographers, and two makeup artists. The job could not be done by one team; it would be from sunrise to sunset, eleven-hour days. I would next see the squad at the Dallas/Fort Worth airport.

This story does not come without complication, however. I was putting final arrangements into place before leaving town for ten days, and I took my last opportunity to take my small dog for an evening walk. A Peekapoo weighing just five pounds and resembling something from Build-A-Bear came to be known as "Teddy," with his blonde, cuddly coat.

It was a mild Texas evening. The relentless heat takes a respite in Fort Worth for a few hours of relief during the p.m. hours. Teddy and I were in the cul-de-sac, headed towards the green belt down the street. Texans are not known for their fences; open spaces are coveted. There were no yard fences separating the residences. "Duke," a Great Dane of grand stature, lived just a few houses away. As I watched in horror, Duke charged, his brown hair bounding towards Teddy, and began to attack him. In defense, Teddy was a flurry, five pounds of lashing, thrashing hair. My only instinct was to intervene. I reached down to separate the two beasts, and in the moment to defend himself, I was bitten by my own dog.

Shaken and trembling, I returned home, covered in blood, clinging onto Teddy and holding him tightly to my chest. Flashbacks flickered in my mind, most certainly PTSD from an earlier time when Beau was killed. Beauregard, a noble name for a teacup poodle weighing no more than a sack of sugar, was attacked by a Scottie of medium size, severing his spinal cord. Beau had to be put down.

I tried to regain my composure, only to realize that I was the one who was bleeding. My only option at this late hour was the Weatherford emergency room. After a thorough cleaning and assessment, the doctor told me that the palm of my left hand would need about five stitches. Now in my sixth month of pregnancy, I was adamant that I did not want to use anesthesia. The doctor met my gaze with a look of apprehension but agreed to stitch my hand using only a topical wipe to dull the pain. I tried to look away as I felt the thread being pulled through my flesh, burning with each tug of the thread, slowly counting backwards from five.

I left the ER department with my left hand throbbing, yet with a sense of relief. It was not my dominant hand, I had received only five stitches, and my dog was not injured. Any devoted pet owner having lived through a previous traumatic death understands that I would not have been able to travel to Cancun had I been forced to relive the death of another dog, "another member of my family."

The airport the following morning was a frenzy of excitement—a sorority sleepover on steroids. The "girls" drew attention everywhere they turned. Long manes of hair moving with the breeze, an ebullience that bubbled over like champagne, and radiant smiles that made you feel as though you had known these women for years. Beauty is an intoxicating element, but the Dallas Cowboy Cheerleaders at the Dallas/Fort Worth airport was newsworthy. Cameras, video cameras, news teams, and airline personnel greeted the squad, which filled the private charter airplane cabin. Bewilderment, however, was also on the faces of a few, wondering what the pregnant lady was doing on the swimsuit shoot. Young women with backgrounds in dance, performing arts, modeling, cheerleading, or a love of the spotlight…and one pregnant lady. It was yet another dichotomy in the span of my career. My left hand now stitched and bandaged, motion sickness patch in place behind my earlobe, and six months pregnant, I boarded the flight from the D/FW airport to Cancun.

We received the same celebrity welcome in Mexico—onlookers hoping to get a candid photo with one of the girls. Their bright eyes sparkled playfully as they flirted with the cameras.

We hit the ground running. With a box of over one hundred swimsuits, the photography began to unfold. Every poolside, beachfront, ocean setting, sunrise, sunset—the goal was to capture thirteen remarkable photos, one for every month of the calendar and the prestigious front cover. It would be several months later that we would photograph the entire squad for the back cover, in my eighth month of pregnancy.

Because I was new on the scene, I had only worked with one of the girls before. Gigi had been to my studio for a makeup lesson, a student of the performing arts and a pageant contestant, and she was the first one in my chair. She was aware of my artistic ability and reputation and did not hesitate to be the first in line. With striking eyes the color of aquamarine and stunning beauty, my work only enhanced her features, and she photographed beautifully against the blue waters of Cancun.

Upon the second day, after the girls became familiar with my work, the line to my chair grew longer. It was an artful dance of professionalism you have to do with another makeup artist on set.

One photo shoot brought us to Ixcarea, to film with the dolphins. The remote locations always added mystique to the setting, in addition to helping with crowd control. To our dismay, an unrelenting tropical storm embraced the small community. The water streaming from the outstretched arms of the palm trees and the pooling puddles on the sand paths made pulling my makeup kit arduous. I made every attempt to favor my left hand while pulling my suitcase with my right hand, through the mud, all the while still trying to smile for the camera crew. The girls were hovering under beach towels, tote bags, and pieces of clothing in an effort to preserve their hair and makeup. As we looked on from a thatched roof and bamboo hut, chickens from a local farmer pecked the ground around our feet.

One young lady stands out in my memory—a very young cheerleader and a rookie to the squad. Her swimsuit had been selected for her, and she came to me with her hair already done, flowing softly around her shoulders. It was another dichotomy, a youthful beauty that was her own worst enemy. She confided in me that she did not have a background in modeling, she didn't know what she was doing, and she didn't know how she had made the cut to be here in Cancun. There were so many others who were more suited to this photo shoot, she felt.

The Cowboys organization had selected a high-cut, two-piece polka dot suit with a built-in bra and halter straps. It looked like something out of a French film in the early 1960s, starring Brigitte Bardot. Game on. These are the artistic moments that I live for, while also hoping to help build someone's self-confidence. I quickly gathered her hair into a messy updo reminiscent of the time period with hairspray and the few hairpins I had in my kit. Tools in hand, sexy black cat-tail eyeliner with false eyelashes, her makeup brought cohesion to the swimsuit and blown out hairdo. By the end of the week, all the girls were asking for false eyelashes.

She asked me if I would help her; she didn't know how to stand or move. The set was a bamboo hut or backdrop, a tropical setting without the water. I asked her to mimic me. I stood in front of her and placed my forearm over my forehead. Now tilt your head this way and twist your body just a bit in this direction. The older, more experienced models knew how to kick into sexy, but she was not yet comfortable in front of a camera.

If you're thinking this sounds a little far-fetched, it's because it was. There we were, the striking beauty of a teenage athlete, with flawless, youthful skin undamaged by time, in a swimsuit—not an ounce of fat on her body—and me, her consultant, at thirty-seven years old, a few short months from delivering a baby. I had to remind myself that I was the expert on beauty. The moment I stepped out of the camera lens' view, I could hear the rapid fire of the camera shutter. When the calendar was printed, she had made the cut. To many it was a surprise. I couldn't have been prouder.

The week concluded with a celebration in a smoke-filled night-club, with lots of dancing and loud music, including coverage from the news magazine entertainment show, *Entertainment Tonight*. My soon-to-be daughter was doing gymnastics in my abdomen. Apparently, she wanted to join in the dancing, too, but I just wanted to retreat to my room and get some dinner and bottled water that wouldn't revolt on me.

As I look through the calendar, I can easily recognize my work from that of the other makeup artist, of which at least 50 percent has "my signature" on it. The calendars of today are no longer shot on location; instead, they are being created in front of a screen. I think back to my trip to Cancun, surrounded by beauty, and appreciate the experience makeup has given me.

Making of the Dallas Cowboys Cheerleaders Calendar - 1994

https://www.youtube.com/watch?v=cpdqM8cj1Rc - part 1

https://www.youtube.com/watch?v=oEfe4Eyu8DU - part 2

https://www.youtube.com/watch?v=lDRwZW2QdAA - part 3

https://www.youtube.com/watch?v=ZSsZZvJ_8hk - part 4

https://www.youtube.com/watch?v=6iMy2GWnIUI - part 5

https://www.youtube.com/watch?v=d1MVN5mB3l8 - part 6

https://www.youtube.com/watch?v=8oOD7cIUvgM - part 7

https://www.youtube.com/watch?v=mOjgYN9M5uk - part 8

Dallas Cowboy Cheerleaders swimsuit calendar shoot – Cancun.

Van Cliburn

"Be Our Guest"

It has been said that artists can be eccentric. Artists might say that the rest of the world is out of step. I remember once working at KTVT news, the Dallas CBS affiliate, to do Joan Rivers' makeup. She was on the phone with Bob Mackey, the legendary fashion designer. He had created a masterpiece for her, and she needed a second ensemble. She travelled with her Yorkie, and certainly Bob could whip something up for the dog, in matching attire, of course! Eccentricity was simply a way of life; nothing to see here.

Feeling as though I were the character from Forrest Gump, I, once again, found myself in odd surroundings. It was a position of wonder. How did I end up in his home, at the dinner table? I had never taken a music lesson, my strengths were not in the fine arts, but here I was, with Van Cliburn, his mother Rildia Bee, and Wendell, having a formal dinner with many courses. I was late night dining with the Fort Worth royalty.

I pulled up to the mansion in Westover. I knew this exclusive community well; it was just a few short blocks from my studio. Many of my clients were from this area. The stately red brick home was tucked away in the manicured landscaping. The bay window and the ornate windows accentuated the time period of the home. The arched double doors created a grand entrance, with its portico suspended securely by two arms of steel into the structure. A lantern sheds light onto the front porch; there is no unnecessary clutter.

I was instructed to pull up to the side entrance and to park along the side of the garage. Upon entering, I could see that I was in a kitchen meant for entertaining. Oversized stainless-steel appliances were lined along the walls, with an island for preparing food. The living space was filled with memories. There were framed photos in every direction you looked—some with rich, gilded trim. Chair rails on the walls, beveled glass doors, and opulent paint choices added to the decadence of the home. Heavy pieces of antique furniture were tastefully arranged. There were chandeliers and heavy draperies. The home was a work of art unfamiliar to me.

What was most striking, I was able to catch sight of his grand piano, and another, and another, and another, and another. There were pianos throughout the multilevel home. At some point I quit counting.

It was late evening, perhaps 9:00 p.m. Typically, I was not called for bookings at this late hour. This was a special occasion. I was asked by Mr. Cliburn to do the makeup for his beloved mother, Rildia Bee. I later came to learn that there was no party, no interview, no photographs, simply a dry run, a trial, to have me do her makeup. I would be applying her makeup for dinner. Wendell, her hairdresser, was also made available.

She was well into her nineties and had a devoted staff. They helped her bathe and dress and assist her in every way that they could. She was playful in personality. After "fussing" at me about the makeup, I placed my hands onto her cheeks. I did not want to force her to wear makeup if she did not want to. I said to her, "Rildia Bee, I'm not hurting you." She turned her face to me, opened her eyes and winked, with a sly smile.

A woman of this generation does not need much makeup; small amounts of moisturizer, foundation, rouge, lipstick, and eyebrows are sufficient. I was not going to risk putting makeup onto her eyes. Wendell removed the curlers from her hair, and her caregivers helped her dress in her brocade two-piece suit and jewelry.

I was given a tour of the property, including the 1952 Chrysler Imperial that was parked in the garage. After winning the first Tchaikovsky International Piano competition in Moscow, New York gave Van a ticker tape parade down the streets of Broadway. This was a celebration typically reserved for Super Bowls, politicians, and dignitaries, not musicians. Van was just twenty-three years of age at the time and thrust into stardom. The car parked quietly in the garage was filled with the ticker tape confetti from 1958.

"You *are* going to stay for dinner, right?"

Now? I thought. *It's well past 11:00 p.m.*

It is not uncommon to be offered a boxed lunch on a jobsite, put out for the crew. I accepted with only slight hesitation, thinking it would be rude not to do so. As I sat down at the long dinner table with upholstered chairs, I joined the family. Their family. His private circle. Dinner with Van Cliburn, Rildia Bee, Wendell, and their caregivers and trusted staff. Roast beef or ham? Mashed potatoes or au gratin? Green beans or broccoli?

It has also been said that artists don't typically work on an eight-hour schedule. They work early morning, well into the evening, in the middle of the night, whatever works best for them. This was Van's schedule, and his household was also on his timeline. Day was night, and night was day. This was not a man who spent his day at the beach.

I glanced around me, feeling like a fish out of water. I wanted to break into song, "Be Our Guest." As I watched for social cues—when to eat, which fork to use—I looked at Van serving himself some vegetables. These are not the hands of a laborer; his skin fair, his nails looking manicured. How many hours must he have spent alone at the piano?

At the conclusion of the evening and well past midnight, it was a "Sunday dinner" long past my bedtime. I smiled as I left that evening, thinking, *Well, that's one for the books.*

My second encounter was more typical, an interview with a local station. What was atypical, however, was that it had appeared that he had been up all night, working, a night owl, in order to make an appearance for the very early day. I applied makeup to his refined features and fair skin, and then raced home to watch the interview on the morning news.

After concluding that the late-night bookings were not practical, I agreed to teach Rildia Bee's caregivers how to apply her makeup for her. I packaged up her merchandise, had it delivered to the Cliburn home, and had the invoice sent in the mail. Soon thereafter, I received a phone call, while in the midst of a busy workday and a studio full of clients.

"Van Cliburn is on the phone."

I took the call in my office and answered, with no indication of what to expect. He was upset, very upset, with his voice raised. He wanted an apology, he declared. I had misspelled his mother's name on the invoice, and it was so disrespectful of me to have done so.

I tried to remain calm, apologizing, and assured him that I did not mean any disrespect, that my office manager had sent the invoice, and that I would be happy to have it corrected. Would he like me to send a second invoice? We concluded the phone call. I took a deep breath, dusted myself off, regained my composure, and rejoined my clients.

I have thought back on that phone call many times, wondering what it was that had so upset him. Was it the misspelling, or was there a deeper meaning? I have to conclude that, due to the adoration and great respect he held for his mother, as his first piano teacher and mentor, it must have been deeply upsetting to see her slipping away. She was cherished, revered, and admired by many around her, as evidenced by the lavish celebrations, public displays of affection, and recognition she received in the Fort Worth circles. Her legacy lives on to this day in the Van Cliburn International Piano Competition, hosting young prodigies from around the world.

Rildia Bee passed away in 1994, at the age of ninety-seven. Van Cliburn passed away in 2013, at the age of seventy-eight.

Lady Bird Johnson

"Southern Hospitality"

She was sitting on the toilet. Here I was, with a former First Lady of the United States, applying makeup to one of the most legendary women of her time, in her powder room.

Let me back up. No, she was not "using" the toilet. Let me be clear on that! But she was seated on her commode, with the lid down, in the small confines of her private bathroom, as I had to almost straddle her to prepare her for an interview, commemorating the Lady Bird Johnson Wildflower Center. My makeup kit was opened on the bathroom sink.

I felt as though I had taken a step back into the 1960s. The charm of an earlier cadence surrounded me. The pastel wallpaper was ornate and timeless. The lighting was just the overhead ceiling fixture, not that of a set in a television studio. The small tiles of the bathroom looked original. Fine paper hand towels were monogrammed with LBJ and set out in the guest bathroom. Shag carpet remains throughout her home. Presidential memorabilia were displayed on mantels and adorned bookshelves and walls.

As I walked through the hallways of what people affectionately refer to as "The Texas Whitehouse," I was in awe. History I had learned as a little girl was now displayed before me in such a personal way. Photos of John F. Kennedy and Lyndon Baines Johnson looked down upon me.

I was escorted to the back of the house, to her personal bathroom right off her bedroom. She was perched on her toilet in a pink bathrobe. Her hair was that of a woman who had just gotten out of bed, matted down and flat. Her eyes glistened like a child on Christmas morning.

"I am so happy to have the woman from Miss America do my makeup and hair," she said, her heavy Southern drawl as thick as honey. My eyes widened as she said this, as I tried to remain calm and not show my alarm. I must be hearing this wrong. *Makeup AND hair?*

The producer had booked this gig just a few short days before the shoot. Dan Rather, a legend in the world of journalism, was again doing the interview with the former first lady. As it turns out, this was just a few years before Lady Bird's passing at the age of ninety-four. I was assured several times, "Not to worry, you will only be doing her makeup. She has a hairdresser." Certainly, there must be a misunderstanding.

On a small set, it is not uncommon to do both hair and makeup. My trade is makeup. Quite frankly, it took the heat off me knowing that I would not be doing her hair. Had I known, I would have come fully prepared! But here I was, with no equipment other than a can of hairspray and a few hairpins. I wondered to myself, *Does a lady in her eighties even own a curling iron?* Straighteners had not yet been invented. I glanced over at Lady Bird's assistant and calmly asked, "Does she have a set of hot rollers we could plug in?"

When I arrived, the lighting and set were done; the small crew of five or six were ready to go. They had the luxury of setting up the previous evening. Because we had such an early start, I made the three-and-a-half-hour drive from Fort Worth to Austin the night before. SIRI was only a twinkle in someone's mind, but the trip was unremarkable. I would be prepping Dan Rather at his hotel that same morning. Dan was a man of integrity and professionalism. It was his job to get the interview, and he would never keep anyone waiting. Ever. I had a job to do, and it needed to be seamless.

I was staying at the same hotel as Dan. This was a smooth process. In my mind, "uneventful" is always a good thing! He greeted me with a smile, I prepared him for the shoot, and I was out of the door.

So here I am, makeup AND hair. The crew is ready to go. "Can she be ready in thirty minutes?" I tried to move in a relaxed manner. I never want the client to feel my stress; they are absorbing the energy from the room. We are making history. It is 7:00 a.m. in Austin, Texas. I already feel my own makeup wilting like a Texas bluebonnet, and I'm sweating like a racehorse after the Kentucky Derby. I glanced at my watch; I got this!

I asked her assistant if there was a current photograph in the home that I could view, to see how she likes to wear her hair. Can I duplicate what she would want? Tools in hand, I was on a mission. I quickly rolled up her hair into the hot rollers, a first for me, applied her makeup, and then continued to work on her hair. I teased and combed, combed and teased, and sprayed. She was a woman of "that decade." Forty-five minutes later, we were done.

I always feel apprehension and excitement at the same time, wondering how a client will see themselves, and more importantly, am I happy with my work? She turned to admire my work in her bathroom mirror and smiled in approval. She did not ask me to make any changes.

In the next room, the crew is unaware of what is transpiring. Dan appears anxious and is standing in the doorway. They don't know that I'm doing two jobs. All they know is that they are waiting, and they are ready to work.

As Lady Bird exited from her bathroom and onto the set, the crew all stood to formally greet the former First Lady. They were audibly and visibly impressed. A murmur fell over the room. Lady Bird moved with the confidence of a beauty pageant contestant. She greeted the all-male crew, and the filming was underway. I exhaled.

The shoot lasted about two hours. I watched from a distance, proud of my work. Lady Bird looked elegant and refined. Her makeup was not that of a presidential ball, mind you. This was classic; she was classic. Her beautiful skin was easy to make "camera ready."

As I am ready to walk away, I quietly shake my head and give myself a pat on the back. How did I manage to pull a rabbit out of the hat? The crew is packing up the set. I pack up my makeup kit. We are done, the interview is a success, and we are about to be on our way.

Lady Bird was from the South, and Southern hospitality was not to be overlooked. She was very polished and gracious and had planned in advance. "Please stay for a traditional lunch of Texas barbeque, and of course sweet tea!" We were all a little surprised by this, but happily accepted. The team was hungry.

As I replayed the morning in my mind, I had to pinch myself. Kudos from the producers and crew, and dining with a happy First Lady. We all gathered in the kitchen to fill our plates; simple, casual, paper plates and napkins, but a moment in history, served up with the grace of a true Southern Belle.

Road Trip - Denver, Colorado 2000

"Missed Opportunity"

The road stretched on for miles. It would be a two-day trip. There was no point in trying to do this drive in one day. I looked over my shoulder to the back seat, and my six-year-old seemed unbothered by the journey. To her, it was an adventure. She was sitting on the passenger side, surrounded by the necessities of life: grapes, string cheese, and the favorite snack at the time, Cheez-Its. She was engaged in a movie on her electronic device, continuously twisting a strand of brunette hair around her finger, seemingly unaware of this soothing habit she had developed. She was neatly tucked in between a pile of books and her favorite blanket.

I had never changed a flat tire before. That was something you called AAA for. Yes, this was the right decision. It would be best to take the longer route, but stay on the major interstates, scenery be damned. 874 miles of interstate. Twelve hours and forty-seven minutes of interstate. The road stretched on for miles.

It was a last-minute decision. Two round-trip tickets from Fort Worth to Denver would be well over a thousand dollars. I would need a car when I arrived. Yes, a late model rental car was the right answer. I decided that the route through the red dirt of Oklahoma and up through Kansas on I-35 would keep me the closest to civilization, rather than going through the panhandle of Texas. If all things went according to plan, we would stay the night in Salina.

My business brought me to Texas. Home and family were in Denver. It was Marion that brought me to Fort Worth, but I knew the customer base in Texas was a good market for me. My business could be successful in the southern part of the country. Women in Denver were prone to hiking, rafting, and skiing. Women in the Dallas/Fort Worth area would not be caught dead going to the grocery store unless they were in a silk blouse and makeup. Over the years things have relaxed a bit, but in the 1990s, this was my cosmetics market.

I had always felt guilty, pulling Shannon away from all her Denver cousins. We missed many playdates, Halloween trick-or-treating, and trips to the mall. I had grown up surrounded by family, and I wanted her to know her relatives. When the idea came up, I wanted to make it happen. She had eleven first cousins in the Denver metro area, and there was going to be a family gathering at the lake. I say, "first cousins," because in Italian families, the family tree goes on for days. We would be celebrating two July birthdays, and since she had never celebrated a birthday with her cousins, Shannon would be included. An October birthday party in July? Why not!

We had been on the road for well over six hours, almost to the halfway point, when the phone rang. I glanced over to the clutter on my passenger seat, looking for my phone. The map was open on the seat, alongside a bag of sunflower seeds. I picked up the flashing phone, recognizing the number on the screen. It was a call from CBS, out of New York. It was July of 2000, George W. Bush had previously announced his candidacy for President of the United States, and the August Republican National Convention was fast approaching.

"Can you be in Austin on Monday to do the makeup for the interview?"

This was a moment that I had only dreamed about. I knew that he was very popular in Texas and that he would most likely be our next President. I looked at the odometer on the dashboard and briefly did some calculations. Today was Friday, and the birthday party at the lake was on Sunday.

"May I call you back in ten minutes?" I said to the producer.

I slowed the rental car, pulled off at the next exit, and pulled over to the shoulder of the highway. I opened the car door and stepped out onto the sun-parched grass along the side of the road. I held my head in my hands, only imagining what this opportunity could do for my career. My stomach began to tighten as I paced back and forth along the length of the car.

"What's wrong, Mom? Are you okay?"

I began the conversation with her, her wide eyes trying to decipher what I was saying. The expression on her face was one that any parent would recognize: confusion, bewilderment, but mostly that of disappointment.

"What about my party? Are we going to have my party?"

I tried to explain to her that this was the man who was probably going to be our next President. CBS was asking me to come to Austin on Monday. This was a big project. I had hoped for this. In the scheme of things, at the end of the road, I knew what I had to do. This birthday party had to happen, and I had to call CBS and turn down the job. It was the first and only time I had declined work with the network. It was a hard pill to swallow.

"Yes, Shannon, you're going to have a party," I reassured her, as I watched the relief wash over her face.

I tried to gather my thoughts before returning the call, slowly pressing the keys with my hesitant fingers. I heard the tone in my voice change from that of excitement to reluctance as I explained the situation to the producer. I wasn't truly confident of my decision until I heard my own voice turning down this opportunity. It was a reality check; I had to surrender to the priorities of motherhood.

It was a glorious day. The sun shone brightly on the ripples of the small lake, with only a slight breeze in the air. The ducks beckoned to be thrown chunks of bread, breaking it into smaller pieces for their ducklings. A turquoise dolphin poster was tethered between two trees, with the words "Happy Birthday" cut out in brightly colored construction paper. My family had gone to a lot of work. The party was everything you could hope for—overcooked hamburger patties on the grill, apple juice boxes spilled onto the sandy beaches, and cousins fighting to read the scavenger hunt map, only to learn that the squirrels had found the candy in the treasure box before they did. It was just as it should be.

Thinking back, if I had taken the time to think it through, I probably could have maneuvered the trip, had my makeup kit flown to Austin, left my daughter in Denver with family, flown to Austin for the job, returned to Denver, only to make the drive back to Texas. It would have been a very expensive decision. I would have lost money had I made that decision. I knew then and I know now that she had to come first. It was a missed opportunity. I had made the decision, and I had to let it go. Perhaps someday I would have the chance to meet George W. Bush, but it was not going to be this day.

The Airbrush - Winter 2000

"A Feather in My Cap, While Eating Humble Pie"

It was the early '90s, and I was in New York for a business trip. While in town, I stopped by CBS for a visit and a tour of the network. I marveled at the oversized portraits of Walter Cronkite and other legends within the industry that lined the hallways. The 1960s were a glamorous time. Black and white photographs displayed Frannie, CBS's makeup artist, in a pencil skirt, bouffant hairdo, stiletto heels, and false eyelashes. The men in the photographs wore skinny ties, and cigarettes burned in the ashtrays like a scene from *Casablanca.*

Frannie was an artist, a pioneer in the makeup room, and she used the simplest of materials to achieve the most results. She began when television was in black and white, travelled with the network, and saw history in the making. Now, watching her work on set, she was showing the passage of time. She had made the decision to retire and pass the torch.

I had been offered the job, but with my studio thriving, I had turned the job down. At that time, I was still hopeful that I would be a mother someday, that I could make rice crispy treats for the kindergarten class, and that my weekends would be filled with swim meets, soccer games, and having quarrels about sunscreen.

Now, in the year 2000, the phone rang in my studio. It was a late-day call.

"LuAnn, you have a call from New York. It's Christina."

"I'll take the call in my office."

Christina introduced herself to me as the makeup artist for CBS. I had been offered a full-time position. Twice. It was an honor to be asked, but I knew that living in New York was not the lifestyle I wanted. The position had been filled. Twice. It didn't work out the first time, the candidate only lasting one year. I knew the position had been filled a second time.

Christina had phoned to talk about airbrush training. I had been travelling with CBS and had established myself with the network, introducing the airbrush when it was in its infancy.

"They've asked me to stop airbrushing him," she said, referring to Dan Rather. "I need to be retrained on airbrush. I need you to train me." I could hear the humility in her voice. There had been a debacle, a miscommunication, really. He said, she said. "We want you to get trained on airbrush," they told her. Fort Worth, Texas, LuAnn Mancini Studios, nor LuAnn Mancini ever entered the conversation. After some research in the trade magazines, she found an airbrush company in Los Angeles that touted their products. She flew to L.A. and took their training. Now, back in New York and after some failed attempts, she was asked about her work.

"What happened? Didn't LuAnn train you?"

"LuAnn who?"

He said, she said.

I questioned whether this was a sound business decision to train Christina. If I trained her, would I no longer receive work from the network? I did not want her job, but would the work go away? They would no longer be tied to me. I had to make a conscious decision. And so, I did, thinking this might open other doors. Maybe I could set up all the affiliates and train all of the news anchors. I looked at it as a way to plant the new seed, a business seed. I had worked for CBS for twenty years, walking onto unknown sets and into unforeseen circumstances. I had checked that box. I had taken my self-taught skills and created a livelihood. I had checked that box, also. Now, they would fly me to New York, paying my expenses and top dollar to train their full-time makeup artist. It would be a feather in my cap.

I arrived in New York, fully anticipating the added pressure. When I walked into the network full of energy and excitement, I felt almost as though I were on display as I was ushered down the hallways and paraded past the many familiar faces and people of distinction. It was again a family reunion welcoming me with open arms, some questioning why I was in New York. It was an out of body experience, again recognizing what I had accomplished. No one questioned my ability… "until I messed up!"

I was immediately taken to the makeup room to meet Christina, located right off the set. The room was small, with a hairdresser's chair that raised and lowered. There were stage lights surrounding the mirror and a counter filled with products.

First impressions speak volumes, and Christina was a woman who could hold her own. She had been raised in Europe, was well travelled, and it was clear she was not easily intimidated. Her broad smile and dimples radiated confidence. While many women rush to the hairdresser to cover their gray hair, her long, striking silver hair framed her face, and she wore it like a badge of honor. It flowed down over her shoulders, adding to her natural beauty. She did not have any children. She was a career person. She was funky and fun, and we immediately clicked.

I asked to see her portfolio. Fully realizing the skill level needed for this job, I was in awe to see her brilliant work. She was a master and sought after as a theatrical makeup artist. I slowly turned the pages of her portfolio, each photograph more stunning than the last, showcasing notable performers within the entertainment industry.

I was overwhelmed when I went through her resume and portfolio that I was there to teach her, training someone who had such a fabulous career and talent. She had worked with elite clientele, the famous of the famous. Stunning costumes, sets, and fantasy makeup using special effects. She was one of the most talented artists I've ever met. Why was I training someone who had so much talent? It was rewarding that they had called me to train her, but I was puzzled.

"This work is so conservative. It's so limiting. I feel like this is trying to fit a square peg into a round hole. Why are you here? Why are you doing the news?"

To no one's surprise, the lifestyle when traveling with rock stars and famous people was a fast and hard career and very demanding. She needed her life to be more structured and stable. She was beginning to get a little older, and she recognized a lifestyle change would be best at this time in her life. I knowingly agreed, reminding myself that I had left my young daughter in Fort Worth for the trip.

I was puzzled why someone with this much talent was having difficulty. As a teacher, I wanted to see what was wrong before I corrected it. I asked Christina to show me what she had used on Dan. Art is not math. One size does not fit all. There's a lot of variables that make it work…or not work.

It didn't take me long to realize the flaws. The compressor was too large and too powerful and dispersed more foundation than was necessary, leaving too much residue on the skin. The silicone foundation was thick and pasty. My foundation was a custom blend. My airbrush was smaller, less powerful, and much easier to control, and CBS was willing to purchase what she needed. It was as if she were trying to water a garden from a fire hydrant.

I went on to teach her airbrush, coincidentally using Mike Wallace as our model. I had to again remind myself this was surreal, acknowledging that our "practice face" was a prominent journalist of seven decades and correspondent for the award winning

60 Minutes show, on his way to film an episode on location that evening.

The lesson continued as we airbrushed Dan Rather, using my familiar products and colors on his face. What wasn't familiar were the robotic HD cameras, lighting, and sound. To this day, I ask myself why I didn't look at the work on the monitor. I ALWAYS check the monitor. Hindsight is 20/20. Yet…I was working with the same face, the same colors—what could be so different, right?

Everything.

After our airbrush lesson, the broadcast begins to take place, and we are in the confines of the control room for one of the best days and one of the worst days of my career. The memory reverberates in my mind to this day.

"Cut."

"Christina! What the f#&k! happened to Dan's left eye?" he barked. It was the first thing out of the executive director's mouth. I was mortified.

There were overhead speakers in every workspace of the CBS network to let the team know when we were on air. We were broadcasting live and had gone to commercial. Anybody that was anybody was in that room. Standing before me was the executive producer. Directly to my left was Christina. The control room felt very small, despite the tiered levels of flooring and multiple monitors above our heads.

The room went silent. It was clear that everyone in the room had heard this comment. All heads turned to look at Christina. She had not done any work on him that day. It was my work, start to finish, as I prepared him for the broadcast and she looked on.

I spoke before having time to think, the words tumbling from my mouth like an overflowing bucket. Yet, given an opportunity to prepare my thoughts and think it through, my words would have been the same.

"It's not Christina. That's my work. I'll correct it, and it won't happen again."

Christina looked at me with an expression of both shock and relief. There was a stunned silence, her expression almost saying, *Thank you.* She had called me, asking for my help. I couldn't let her take the fall for my work. At that point a bond was developed, because of the integrity that we shared.

I finished up the day's work and packed up my kit, hailing a cab back to the hotel. I had no desire to see Manhattan. I was broken. Everything was flashing before me.

I sat in the tub of my hotel room, the hot water filled to the brim and enveloping my body. I lamented the events of the day, sobbing until there was nothing left to expel, my head now throbbing, and my eyes swollen.

Am I qualified? Am I adequate? Is this good enough? I had to give myself a pep talk and overcome this. Poverty teaches you a lot of things; among them, creativity, perseverance, and resilience. What you don't have, you create. What you want to get from life, you struggle for. When you fail, you get back up. I had to get back up.

I ordered room service, Caesar salad and a cold beer, only to push the pieces of romaine lettuce around the plate. If "humble pie" had been on the menu, I would have ordered it. I said a prayer of good night and asked to wake up renewed, to be able to walk into the studio with confidence and nail it—for Christina, for me, for all of my associates.

The following morning, I walked into the CBS studio, wanting to exude an air of confidence.

"Show me what you use under his eyes," I asked Christina with enthusiasm.

She taught me a trick using a theatrical makeup technique, and I went on to teach her about the airbrush. We worked together, each preparing half of a face. To our relief, the day concluded without incident, and the producers were pleased with the work.

Christina's path and my path crossed several times in the future, two professionals in the field. It was exciting to see her work evolve and blossom into her fantasy makeup and stage makeup, using the fundamentals from our session that day. The airbrush only enhanced her natural talent and allowed her abilities to soar. There was never any tension between us, only that of mutual respect and trust. I had overcome the obstacle and was able to sign off on the assignment before me. Little did I know this was going to become more than just an artistic accomplishment. It was a life lesson.

Air Force One - Waco, Texas:
One-Year Anniversary of 9/11

"Forever Changed"

If you are old enough, you remember vividly where you were on that fateful morning when you heard the news, saw the broadcast, or saw the news scrolling across your cell phone screen with the breaking story. September 11, 2001, America was forever changed. The Twin Towers in New York City, the Pentagon, the plane crash in Pennsylvania. Everyone remembers where they were.

I was in my bedroom with the television on in the background. It was shortly before 8:00 a.m. in Fort Worth, Texas, and I was scrambling to get my six-year-old daughter to school by 8:30. Breakfast would have to take place in the car, she could buy her lunch from the school cafeteria, and I could get to my studio by 9:00 a.m. At 8:46 a.m. Eastern Standard Time, America was forever changed.

Like the rest of the world, I froze in place, dumbfounded and numb. There was a terrorist attack on our nation. Do I take her to school? Will the schools be closed? My mind was spinning, trying to decipher what to do first. I went through the motions and drove to our nearby elementary school. I pulled away from the carpool line, feeling relieved that I did not have to answer the questions on the young faces of the students or try to calm the older children. My mind was churning as I absentmindedly drove to the studio. The short commute seemed interminable as I listened to the news on the radio, desperately wanting to get to the studio to turn on the television set and learn more.

When I arrived, it was eerily quiet. Makeup was the last thing on the minds of my customers. I was unsettled all day long. The phone did not ring on 9/11. In the days that followed, I remember thinking that the skies went silent. There was no sound from overhead travel, and there was very little traffic on the roadways.

One year later, shortly before the anniversary of the attack, I was getting ready to board *Air Force One*. Scott Pelley would be interviewing the four pilots who ensured the safety of President Bush. I made the two-hour drive south to the Waco Regional Airport, a small airport that was easily accessible when President Bush needed to travel from his Prairie Chapel Ranch in Crawford, and an easy commute for *Marine One*.

From a distance, the airport appeared bucolic, the simple patterns of the runways dividing the landscape. The majesty of *Air Force One* sat on the runway, its pale blue exterior matching the Texas skies. Alongside the aircraft were the wingmen, two F-16 fighter planes. What must have been commonplace to the town of Waco seemed oddly awry to me, to see this spectacle, *Air Force One*, sitting on the runway of this small airport.

Security was high. Fearing another attack on the anniversary, I was greeted by bomb-sniffing canines and Secret Service agents with their wands. Once the CBS team had completed the process and had been cleared through security, we were allowed to board the aircraft to prepare for the documentary.

I was hopeful that this might be the day that I would get to meet the President. If he was on *Air Force One* that morning, I was unaware of it. It was yet another "brush with Bush."

When I entered the plane, I felt as though I had boarded a cruise ship, with its leather sofas lining the windows. The small porthole windows were symmetrically spaced along the walls, and there were several table lamps strategically mounted onto the built-in tables and seating areas. The neutral colors of the cabin provided a calm-ing atmosphere.

I was shown to a small boardroom to wait for the crew to set up for filming and found it odd that I was left alone in this sacred place. As I looked around, I sat with my arms folded, scouring the room. I had hoped there might be some small remnant that I could take with me, to validate that I had been on *Air Force One*. A magazine, a notepad, a water bottle, a napkin, or paper cup. Something that bore the emblem or Presidential seal.

I was seated for two or three minutes, although it felt like much longer. As I'm waiting for the pilots to arrive, I feel the presence of someone's eyes on me. I turn to look, and there's a man I assumed to be military personnel standing behind me. I felt my face blush, but nonetheless had to ask, "Is there anything at all on this plane that I could have as a souvenir? Something that I could show to my daughter and her sitter? They always love hearing the stories."

He smiled knowingly, having heard this request before. "Let me look around." One minute later, he returns with a book of matches with the Presidential seal. He also had in his hands an iconic box of chocolate M&Ms, apparently a favorite of President Bush. The box had the Presidential seal on it. *Wow,* I thought. *That's a feather in the cap for Hershey's!*

After completing the makeup for the four pilots, my work was done. I was unable to see the interview live; it was done in a secured space. But I was able to enlist the help of the security guard, and he graciously gave me a quick tour of the public spaces on the plane. *Air Force One* was a double-decker, including a boardroom with cap-tain's chairs and monitors, gold coasters, and leather-bound tables. It did not feel like an airplane, or at least the economy class that I know all too well. The master bedroom was towards the back of the plane. I peeked through the doorway into the master bedroom but did not step inside. That would have felt like an invasion of privacy. The pilots' quarters were much like that of an RV, located near the cockpit, with bunk beds and a small table for eating or a workspace for computers.

I drove home that morning, once again completing my workday well before noon. The documentary aired on Sept. 8, 2002, on CBS *60 Minutes II*. I watched in horror as I learned details reserved for classified ears, later to be made public. The President was feared to have been a target for another attack. Vice President Cheney was swept off to a bunker for his safety. With four pilots on board, they were prepared to stay airborne for as long as necessary. At one point, the President demanded that he be taken to the nearest base airport so he could publicly address the nation.

Almost 3,000 lives were lost that day. The nation was left reeling, feeling broken hearted and helpless, yet united and patriotic in a twisted juxtaposition. I knew at that time that September 11, 2001 would change our way of life for generations to come.

Wendell Abbott - 1954–2005

"Unexpected Visitor"

It would be sudden and unpredictable. *"1-800-Serendipity."* He never planned anything. He refused to live his life like that.

I received a call on my cell phone. Had I heard? It was a Sunday morning. He had been having brunch at the Worthington Hotel. He stepped away from the table to visit the gift shop. There were sirens.

I spoke with Frank, the owner of the salon where Wendell worked. I needed to know more. It was sudden and unpredictable. He did not suffer. Wendell and I had a shared faith and believed in the afterlife. When God came to call, he was ready.

I attended the viewing and the funeral services and sat in the back. I was still in shock. It was standing room only. I looked into the casket. Wendell would have been pleased with the way he looked.

The man spoke about Wendell's life in very black and white terms. He was born in Calipatria, California, a small town one hour north of the Mexico border. His mother had died at an early age with the same genetic heart condition that he had inherited. He was raised by his father, amongst a pack of brothers in a Christian home. It was a meager existence. He was a country boy.

Wendell and I shared a journey together. We met as young entrepreneurs, booked weddings together, and spent many hours backstage. He was by my side, watching my daughter grow up. He always found pride in spending time with her, never correcting strangers that assumed he was the father. He threw a party for my fortieth birthday, and he brought me a puppy when I had suffered a devastating loss of my dog. Wendell always told me how beautiful I was. He supported me through weight loss, even though he loved me for who I was. He was my shoulder to cry on through my divorce and my greatest cheerleader when others were not. Wendell and I would tolerate each other's idiosyncrasies. We laughed, we cried, we argued.

The last time we spoke was an argument. It was a falling out that we never reconciled. He didn't want any more business. He didn't need any more business. Don't send any more referrals. Two weeks later, he found himself sitting next to his past client at the opera, with a new haircut and color. It was not his work. He was livid.

I sat in the small hair salon with a cape around my shoulders, both of us raising our voices for all to hear. He applied the color to my hair as we continued to argue.

"Wendell, you told me you did not want any more business. Can't we talk about this? Let's step outside and talk. You are out to lunch!"

This set him off, and he said, "No, I'm done with you. Somebody else can do your hair."

He became so angry with me that he walked out, leaving me with a head full of hair dye and the door slamming behind him. I felt sure that all of Fort Worth heard about this spat.

I thought he would cool down, sleep on it, and it would be over. It snowballed. We did not speak, time slipped away, and he passed away a little over a year later. Wendell would have said, "Don't let the noise get in the way," yet we did.

The days passed, and we all grieved the loss of Wendell. He left a lasting memory of a giving soul, someone who devoted himself to building the esteem of others.

I arrived at my studio one Tuesday morning to find my staff preparing for the day.

"Did you leave all of the lights on yesterday?"

"I may have left a light on."

"No. ALL of the lights. They were on when I arrived," Laurie said. I dismissed it as a fluke.

Wednesday morning brought another occurrence. When the staff arrived, the music on the sound system was on. Not simply left on, but blaring pop music.

People have different beliefs, whatever they may choose to call them. Some refer to their faith and the afterlife—angels and the golden gates of Heaven—and others may call it ghosts or spirits.

The energy was not negative, but the oddities left me to wonder. Each morning I arrived at my studio on Byers Avenue wondering what I might find. By the second or third day I thought to myself, *Wendell must be visiting. He's such a prankster. I wonder what he's trying to tell me.*

Thursday morning, all of the fabric covered chairs from the manicure station were pushed into the lobby area of the studio.

By Friday, my staff was on edge, apprehensive to enter the studio alone. We had leftovers in the fridge from the previous day. We all typically use the metal utensils from the kitchen drawer, yet there was a plastic fork left in the food.

What is it I am supposed to pay attention to? What is he trying to tell me? Why was I getting this unexpected visitor?

On the fifth day, I had an appointment with a client I hadn't seen in twenty years. She was a real estate agent in the area and unexpectedly ended up on my appointment book. She sat in my chair as I prepared her makeup, and we talked casually.

"Oh, by the way. I'm in charge of Wendell's property. His estate sale is this weekend."

I smiled, now knowing what Wendell was trying to tell me. "Now I understand why you're here. Got it." She smiled at me, not questioning my sanity.

I reminisced and cried, not feeling mentally prepared to be in his home and amongst his personal belongings. Why would I go? Why would I need to go? Closure. To have closure and reconcile our differences.

It was midday on a hot Sunday morning. I pulled through the gate and into the circle drive, just a ten-minute commute from my studio. The stately brick ranch style home sat on a plot of land, set back from the street. A Model-T invited car enthusiasts to come closer.

Located behind the home was a small barn, with goats and chickens. Wendell had been a country boy at heart. I could only envision him feeding the chickens in his bare feet. He hated wearing shoes.

On the property sat a large motorhome for road trips to escape the trappings of the city.

It felt odd to see strangers wandering through his home, picking amongst his belongings, invading his private space. What I found most striking was that within the facade, in every direction I turned, I saw the finest crystal and china that money could buy. Original artwork and hand-crafted furniture were everywhere I looked. I made my way into his bedroom, feeling like a patron in a Neiman Marcus showroom. I continued to delve into his solitude and slowly looked through his wardrobe. His fine silk shirts hung neatly aligned, with the designer labels all facing the same direction, like a platoon of soldiers. The collars were buttoned at the top button and hung wrinkle free in the closet. Fine leather shoes lined the floor in tidy pairs.

Within the back mud room, Wendell had kept his hair supplies—his brush, bobby pins, and a blow dryer, which brought a smile to my face.

I selected a small crystal ashtray to buy. Additionally, I purchased a silver ring that Wendell always wore. I was about to leave when I ran into one of our mutual friends. We conversed, shared stories, teared up, and then openly cried. She held out her hand, also exposing a silver ring that belonged to Wendell.

Wendell had found a path in which he could live in a small-town way in a big city. Somebody who lived such a short life lived from zero to 100 in his time on this Earth. He began with nothing and ended up with everything. No rules. No regrets. Not many people can say that.

I drove away after being allowed into Wendell's private world. More importantly, I got to say goodbye. Maybe this was Wendell's way of letting me know that he forgave me, but what I regret most is that I did not fight harder to forgive him.

Wendell W. Abbott, 50, passed away Sunday, June 26, 2005, in Fort Worth.

Funeral: 1:30 p.m. Thursday in Greenwood Chapel. Entombment: Independence Chapel, Greenwood Mausoleum.

Wendell W. Abbott was born Aug. 6, 1954, in Calipatria, California. He will be remembered for his generosity and kindness to a myriad of family and dear friends.

Published in *Star-Telegram* from June 29 to June 30, 2005.

My dear friend, Wendell.

George W. and Laura Bush - November 2009–2013

"Down Home"

After a long-awaited decade, several encounters brought me into the Bushes' sphere. My first introduction to Laura Bush was in 2009, during a brief makeup touch-up at the Dallas Civic Center, honoring her for her work in the arts. I got the sense that Laura Bush did not like makeup. Some women relish the occasion to have makeup done by a professional, adoring the attention, glamour, pampering, and everything that surrounds it. Laura Bush was not one of those women.

The second occasion was a busy Saturday afternoon in my Fort Worth studio. I was hired by a bride, never having met her before. The wedding was going to take place at a prestigious Fort Worth landmark. As I'm preparing her makeup for her wedding that same day, I learn that she is an assistant to Laura Bush, and that George W. and Laura Bush were two of her honored guests.

I wondered to myself, can someone of this stature attend a wedding without drawing attention to themselves? Will there be a political protest going on to distract from the wedding? Will this appearance result in a story on the evening news? How difficult it must be living such a public life, hoping to catch a glimpse of their prior selves.

As I was doing the makeup for the bride, I even joked with her, "Everyone has that one uncle, that one brother, that one cousin, that one guest that you need to keep away from the former President, for fear of them trying to make a political statement or have their voice heard. Thankfully, the bride and groom celebrated the day without incident, and the Bushes remained unscathed. I mused that while in the shadow of proximity to the Bush family, I hadn't yet had the opportunity to work with them. Perhaps this event, this wedding, would open some doors for me, professionally. Word of mouth or a referral might come my way. At the end of the day, I still did not get the chance to meet two members of the Texas royalty.

It had now been ten years since the birthday party road trip to Denver. It was a call I thought I would never again receive. Time had, once again, repeated itself, and I would at long last be doing makeup for the former President.

It was November 2010 in Dallas, Texas, a beautiful time in the South, with shades of auburn, crimson, and gold filling the out-stretched branches of the trees. It was 6:00 a.m., and the sun was just about to rise above the tree line. I pulled into the exclusive community where Laura Bush and George W. lived, in an attempt to keep a low profile and get back to normalcy following his two terms in office. Although this was his post-presidency, the Secret Service greeted me in an unmarked SUV with an imposing air. An agent who lived in the corner property, with a manner of caution and a flashlight, asked for a photo ID.

"I'll bet you know more about me than I know about myself. I'll bet you know my daughter's name," I said in jest to the agent dressed in street clothes. With only a slight smile and acknowledgement of my sense of humor, I was allowed to proceed into the cul-de-sac near the Bush property.

The ranch home was set back off the street, stretching across the acreage. The brick home was surrounded by mature trees, with the remains of summer unwilling to surrender. Although it was stately in many regards, what struck me most were the two flag poles in the yard, with lights projecting upward to illuminate both the United

States flag and the Lone Star State flag. Full-length shutters framed the windows, and two lanterns embraced the front entry door. The manor that the Bushes now call home has been described as "a bit smaller"; to them, it must have been a welcome change from the grandeur of the White House.

As I stepped into the home, the open layout of the floorplan showed an appreciation for the "out of doors." The view of the back of the property could be seen from the foyer. Two black Scotties, properly groomed and trained, were lying at attention, so much so that they appeared to be porcelain statues, moving only when commanded to do so. As cameramen, tech crew, and strangers to the home came and went, they were canine soldiers only wanting to please.

The home was pristinely clean yet welcoming in such a way that I wanted to sit for a cup of tea and never leave. The contemporary finishes were sleek, with beautiful artwork, rugs, and furniture displayed in a space with lots of windows and light.

The interview of George W. was to take place with Jim Axelrod to air on CBS *Sunday Morning*, in celebration of the publication and new book release of *Decision Points*. I was shown to the guest powder room, through a long corridor. Like any doting parents, no different because they had lived in the White House, the walls were lined with photos of their two twin daughters, Barbara and Jenna.

The powder room was confining. Because I didn't want to have a replay of the confines of an enclosed area like that of Lady Bird Johnson, I asked his aide if we could have a stool brought in. Although the quantity of cosmetics is fewer with a male, I meticulously set up my makeshift makeup station on the vanity of the sink. He stepped into the small space, comfortable in his skin, with a broad smile. Now at sixty-four years old, he was lean and appeared fit. I stood waiting with my makeup cape draped over my arm, ready to greet the former President.

"I'm LuAnn Mancini. Welcome to my salon," I said jokingly, as I greeted the 43rd President.

"Hi, I'm George W.," he replied, with his Southern humor, aware that an introduction was not needed.

"Do you mind makeup, Mr. President?"

"Just make me look as good as you can."

I immediately felt at ease with George W. I think that, perhaps, he was my favorite client over the span of my thirty-five-year career. There was no hidden agenda. When he spoke, his earnest eyes met my eyes. He spoke directly to me, making note of details that he could recall years later.

I draped the cape around his body and used Kleenex on his collar to ensure that there would be no makeup residue. I prepared to airbrush his skin as I casually asked, "Do you have contacts in?"

Laughing openly, he replied, "I don't have contacts out."

I began to airbrush his skin as we spoke comfortably. He was cordial, asking many questions about me. I shared with him that I had a makeup salon.

"How is business? Has Texas been good for your business?"

"Yes, Texas has been good to me."

Conversation was easy, and it was at this time that I felt obliged to carry out a promise I had made to my daughter.

"Mr. President, I have a sixteen-year-old daughter, Shannon, who is in high school. She LOVES you and she made me promise that I would tell you. She begged me to come today to meet you, but I told her that was not possible."

Before we had completed the conversation, he immediately waved for his aide. The President was handed a notecard and pen, which he signed, "To Shannon, Best Wishes, George W. Bush." Along with the signed note, he handed me two lapel pins with the Presidential seal, encased in small blue boxes. On the back was his embossed signature. One for mama and one for daughter. I was immensely grateful.

Later that day, I pulled into the parking lot of the high school with an afterschool snack from Chick-Fil-A, a sweet tea, and a personally hand-signed gift from the 43rd President. One foot in one world, one foot in another. At the time of writing this book, Shannon is now in law school. I expect that I will see the framed notecard in her law library someday.

Southern Methodist University - January 2013
"The Library"

I stepped into the oval office, or so I thought. As I exited the private second floor elevator, I was entering a replica of the White House. The striped satin chairs, the circular rug on the inlaid wood floor, and the Presidential portraits mimicked the Washington, D.C. landmark. George W. was gracious and humble as he shared his new library, his museum, and his private office with Bob Schieffer, the CBS journalist. Laura could not have been more proud to have served as the honorary chairperson for the building. Despite its grandeur, through the efforts of remarkable fundraising efforts, the Presidential Library would already be paid for upon its upcoming christening.

George W. - April 2013

"Dedication"

It was an occasion reserved for inaugurations, funerals, and ceremonies of great distinction. The dedication of the George W. Bush Presidential Library located on the Southern Methodist University campus would bring together five living presidents and five first ladies.

The preparation was immense, including a one-on-one private interview with George W., leading up to the formal ceremony. I was hired shortly before the interview, out of New York, to do the makeup for Charlie Rose, the broadcast journalist.

She was "snubby," the producer out of New York. "We need you to do makeup for Charlie Rose. We've secured a private interview with George W. Bush, and we need you to do Charlie's makeup."

"What about the President?" I inquired.

"No, no, no. He's not going to want makeup."

Okay, I thought. *You're going to put the President on national television without makeup? I've already done his makeup.* I was the "local girl." She worked in New York.

It was a 6:00 a.m. call. Typically, makeup is set up near the cameras, on set, to ensure efficiency, but I was instructed to set up down the hall. Way down the hall. Go down the hall to do Charlie's makeup. Charlie Rose greeted me with an air of distinction. At the time he was a "somebody," at the top of his game. Now, on set, makeup ready, mic'd up and ready to go, he stood awaiting George W.

As if on cue, in walks George W. and greets the room. Easy in his nature, he smiles at the crew, walks directly to my station, and sits down in my chair. He had become quite accustomed to these events and the protocol, and he did not hesitate to settle in for me to apply his makeup.

I smiled at him, without seeking further approval or confirmation, and with the bravado of a bullfighter, I draped the cape around him. We began to chit-chat like old friends. There was a stunned silence in the room.

"How is your daughter?"

"Shannon is great. She's now attending Texas A&M."

We conversed effortlessly. I used the lint roller on his suit for a last-minute touch up, and off he went for the interview. I smiled at his ease, his formal yet polite interactions with women, and the way he interacted with men. He was a guy's guy, appearing most at ease within a group of men. If I didn't know any better, I would say that he was in a barbershop, chatting with his oldest and dearest friends. He always appeared to be in the moment.

In a 2014 CBS *Sunday Morning* interview, the former President speaks about his father, George Herbert Walker Bush. He is quoted as saying, "One of the unique strengths of George Bush is he had the capacity to put himself in the other fellow's shoes." The same could be said of George W.

After the completion of the interview, the former president, Charlie Rose, and almost the entire crew assembled for the class photo. Almost everyone. I was not asked to be in the photo. As the photo concludes, George W. turns and walks down the hallway towards me.

"Do you want a picture?"

He knew what was going down and the hierarchy that ensued. While others looked on, following the group photo, I took a solo photo with No. 43. Just him and me. It was the little subtleties that he picked up. He was the man of importance, yet he made me feel important.

We snapped a photograph, I quickly took off his makeup, packed up, and walked to the car at 9:30 a.m., my entire workday already done. I would go back to my world, and he would go on to his world. I always found these moments to be both intoxicating and perplexing; one foot in one world, one foot in another.

President George W. Bush

LuAnn Mancini - 2009

"Crazy Cat Lady"

"**P**lease don't tell anyone what you're doing," she begged. My daughter looked at me in exasperation, wondering how we found ourselves to be the landlords of, now, nine cats. She was a sophomore in high school, concerned about what her peers might think about her mom, the "Crazy Cat Lady."

My life has never been conventional. My career path has not been conventional. So, too, was the episode of taking back the neighborhood. Most people would not call our plan "conventional."

We lived in the quiet neighborhood of Benbrook, a suburb where the homeowners spend their weekends doing yard work, children ride their bikes in the cul-de-sac, and you know your mailman by his first name.

My neighbor came to visit one afternoon. We were mailbox neighbors, only meeting to exchange a few pleasantries. She sauntered across the street, still in her work clothes, ready to put on her "sensible shoes." The Texas heat was oppressive, even after the sun sat low on the horizon.

I was on my knees, working in the flower bed, adding to my pile of dandelions. I am not what most people would call a gardener, and I welcomed the distraction. I tossed my gardening gloves onto the hot ground and stood to wipe the sweat from my forehead.

"We have a problem in the neighborhood," she said.

"What do you mean?" I queried, seeing the concern in her expression.

"Have you not seen all of these feral cats?"

Our neighborhood was being overrun. Not by gangs, not by trash, not by overgrown and unkept yards. It was being overrun by cats, like a scene from a third-world country. One female cat, in particular, and two male cats that kept her company. The three cats were feral, yet had captured the compassion of my neighbor. "Mama" had made herself welcome and would scavenge from her back porch cat bowl, and now the two male companions were making themselves at home, as well. And when the time came to deliver her next litter, she would find her way to the abandoned motorboat across the street, tuck herself away in the hull filled with fallen leaves from the trees, and deliver the next set of residents to our block.

And so it began, a strategic plan between my neighbor and me. Finding homes for all of the offspring was challenging enough, but the problem would not be solved unless we first addressed the issue of having the "ring leaders" spayed and neutered. We agreed that if I were the one to house the cats and place them into homes, she would cover the expenses. Without fully realizing what I was getting myself into, I drew the short straw. I was a pet lover, but I did not consider myself a cat person. I always loved dogs. *How was I the one tasked for this job?*

We devised a plan. She would take care of the adult cats. Trap, neuter and spay, have them vaccinated, and then they could be returned to the neighborhood. I would take care of the kittens.

My neighbor owned a live trap and acquired a second trap. Cat lovers or not, we did not want to harm these orphans. After three trips to the veterinarian for preventive surgeries, mama cat and her two rogue mates were off the market. Agenda item number one, accomplished.

Agenda item number two: capture, tame, and place many cats into adoptive homes. This was easier said than done. The older litters were accustomed to living on the street and were very elusive, yet the newborn kittens were easy prey. The mother cat would eventually leave her babies for short periods of time to scavenge for food within the neighborhood, and this was my window of opportunity.

On summer days, the young felines would peek their small faces above the side of the boat and bask in the warm sun on its outer rim. Once I knew the kittens were being weaned, I would watch, stalk, and pounce. When she would leave the litter unattended, I would stealthily creep up on the boat, reach over the side, grab a kitten by the nape, and make my getaway.

I found myself unexpectedly mourning for the mama cat, coming home to find her little ones gone. How must she feel? I had to convince myself that this was in the best interest of these creatures. The average life expectancy of a feral cat on the streets is less than two years, while domestic cats can live over twenty years.

I became known as the cat whisperer, at least in my own mind. These were wild cats. Although I was talked into adopting two domestic cats when my daughter was in second grade, these street cats were not loveable, purring, human companions. These were hissing, spitting, clawing balls of matted fur. At times I found myself chasing cats around my home, the felines scurrying, defensive, and huddled underneath my bed. I survived cat scratch fever and spent hours upon hours cleaning cat boxes and vacuuming cat litter from the carpet.

I was fascinated by these homeless creatures, trying to understand their psyche. It became a systematic process of trying to break the cycle, trying to substitute fear of humans for love of human touch. It was a matter of patience and trying to earn their trust. I staged the cats into different rooms of my home, based on their development. With a trusted bath towel as my armor, I would swaddle the kittens, and I would hold, stroke, brush, and love on these cats several times a day. I held them close to my chest, so they could hear my heartbeat and feel my breath. At first it was a battle of wills, with very noncompliant subjects. After time, they had no choice but to surrender. Eventually they could run around a contained room, and finally have full run of the house.

Having lived on the streets, the cats were all very motivated by food. Once they were allowed to be outdoors, it was literally a cattle call for dinner. I would ceremoniously step outside onto the driveway with a can and metal spoon and clang the container, and my subjects would come scurrying from the bushes for their evening meal. If you didn't know better, it looked like a scene from a Friskies cat food commercial.

I was very selective of prospective families. These little beings were scarred and untrusting of people. One family came to visit, hoping to adopt and excited to meet their new four-legged family member. They had a young preschool daughter, and she had never had a pet before. After assessing the interaction, I declined the family, suggesting that they might visit PetSmart for their new pet. Their young daughter was too young, a little too exuberant, and the cat had a skittish temperament, remaining in my lap and on my shoulders during their visit. "This is not her best starter cat."

I often felt like a character in my own book, living in two different worlds. At my studio, the walls were lined with photos of beauty queens, celebrities, and politicians, while at the same time the bulletin board in the kitchen of the studio was lined with photos of cats looking for potential homes. One by one, I was able to adopt them out, sometimes two or three per weekend. Many of my neighbors adopted a cat, so many cat siblings and cousins remained in the neighborhood. The matriarch of the cats also remained in the neighborhood, but the two male cats moved on like wayward sailors.

And then there were three. A three-year mission that I did not anticipate. Three family members happily seeing this mission come to a close. And now we were the owner of three more cats, in addition to our original two domestic felines. I don't think anyone would second guess that I have earned the name of "Crazy Cat Lady."

Laredo

"Hazardous Materials"

If I were any closer to Mexico, I could reach across the border and touch it. Laredo mirrors Corpus Christi on the latitudinal planes, yet sits squarely landlocked on the border between Texas and Mexico. It is a community that is so close to the border crossing that it is hard to recognize that you're not already in another country.

The Rio Grande River divides the two worlds—a small body of water moving with only a slight current, many having been fooled by its undercurrent. It is no wonder that lives are lost every year, people trying to escape the adversity of their birthplace, trying to cross over, leaving behind them the destiny of impoverishment. Both the American flag and the Mexican flag are waving.

From the security of their booths, border agents can view the throngs of people in their cars atop the blistering black asphalt, which creates a mirage in the rippled atmosphere. Trucks with varying license plates wait for inspection—some patiently, some less so. People on foot walk across the imaginary line, work visas in hand.

Our hotel looked down upon the green waters of the Rio Grande. At night you could hear the barking that resonates from the dog kennels at the water's edge, signaling signs of unrest.

"Rather" was doing a story on gang violence and crime at the border, resulting in family members being erased from humanity. Tonight there would be a stakeout—investigative work to interview people willing to speak anonymously to the press; these would be people with family in the U.S., families of victims, and gang members hoping to escape their troubled existence.

Before leaving for the streets of Nuevo Laredo across the Mexican border, we gathered at the police department to first interview the police chief. It was not a job for the faint of heart. A former chief of police had been on the beat just over seven hours before being killed by gang members. I felt uneasy as I watched Dan suit up in his bulletproof vest. It seemed ironic that this morning I had applied powder to his face for the interview, yet now he was preparing to go into the streets of Mexico to meet with victims of gang violence. I was equally disturbed as I watched the police arm themselves with the arsenal of guns sitting on the table before us.

The crew asked if I wanted to go on the stakeout. It was a dangerous time. No, I decided. I'll sit in the security of my hotel room on this side of the border and watch a pay-per-view movie. I don't need to be a hero and witness a crime tonight.

Having ordered my Caesar salad from room service, I felt like a hypocrite having drawn the lucky straw and having been born of second-generation immigrants. I now have a better understanding of why these immigrants wanted to be on this side of the river. It seemed so simplistic, yet so extreme. From my balcony and bird's-eye view, I could look in one direction and see the amber waves of grain. If I look in the opposite direction, I can see the waters that serve as a passageway for the "illegals." I felt lucky to be an American.

On the last day of filming, I finished up work and headed out for my flight. I would travel to the D/FW Airport and drive home to Fort Worth, and the CBS crew would connect on to New York. I again felt unsettled as I noted the heightened security in the airport, with military style guns on display from the soldiers who stood on guard. There was a stark difference between the Laredo International Airport, located on the border, and that of D/FW.

I casually checked in, walked down the corridor to board my flight, and waved to greet my coworkers as I boarded the plane. They were seated up front in first class, and I would be seated towards the rear of the cabin, in coach.

Airplane travel remains high on my list of things I'd rather avoid, right alongside getting a root canal and going to the gynecologist. I checked the seat pocket in front of me for the motion sickness bag, preferring to think of it as a doggie bag for leftovers. With my scopolamine patch in place behind my ear, maybe I wouldn't need it this time. I glanced through the in-flight magazines that were located in the seat pocket in front of me and considered purchasing all of the things I didn't know I needed. I was glad I had picked up the latest edition of *People* magazine.

Settling into the seat, I tried to get comfortable against the stiff vinyl and heard my name come over the loudspeaker. I stepped into the aisle, inconveniencing my neighbor a second time, and went to the front of the cabin to inquire.

"LuAnn Mancini? We need you to exit the plane and go back to the ticket counter."

I again acknowledged my colleagues in first class as I was escorted off the plane. They looked at each other with a slight bit of confusion, and I smiled, a bit puzzled.

"Good luck…" they said, as their voices trailed off.

I followed the flight attendant, wondering whether I had mistakenly left my wallet or ID at the counter and hoping I was going to make it back onto the plane in time for takeoff. I was instructed to leave the secured area and go back to the check-in ticketing counter in the main terminal.

I hastily made my way to the ticket counter and was greeted by a couple of security people standing there, feeling their eyes make a quick pass up and down my body. *Is this our terrorist?* I recognized my floral tapestry bag in front of them. I was informed that they had "detected explosive material" in my luggage and were going to go through it now. In the middle of this escapade, I didn't give it much thought. Looking back on this episode, it seemed odd to me, seemingly careless, that if there had been explosive materials in my luggage, they would examine my bag in the middle of a crowded airport.

One of the agents held a wand like a magic scepter, which he used to hover over my bag. He scanned the piece of luggage in systematic rows, in multiple directions, from every imaginable angle. It beeped and lit up like fireworks on the 4th of July.

Am I in trouble? I thought to myself.

"Step back, ma'am.

"Do you want me to help you open it—

"Step back, ma'am."

I looked on as they unzipped the length of the suitcase. I had purchased some stick matches at the local drugstore, without giving it much thought. Now, watching the TSA agents pull them from my bag, I began to feel uneasy. Fearing this might look suspicious, yet giving it further thought, I didn't understand why this would have been a problem, having packed them in my luggage. They continued to rummage through my belongings, as I felt the minutes ticking away until my flight was scheduled to depart. To make matters worse, he sees the air compressor for my airbrush, wondering what sort of purpose this machine could serve.

In a frenzy of nerves as I watched this scenario unfold, combined with the distinct possibility that I was about to miss my flight, I began to talk, babble really, like popping popcorn overflowing its kettle.

"I was at the police station last night for a stakeout. There was a stockpile of loaded guns on the table. Maybe some gunpowder could have gotten on my suitcase? Maybe while I was in the police station someone planted something in my suitcase. Maybe I was set up?"

I see the wrinkled expressions on their face, wondering what kind of can of worms they may have opened. *Was I going to become the story?*

After a brief inspection, they noted that my luggage was saturated, soaked and wet. One of my skin toners was empty, the lid was loose and had leaked all over the suitcase. There was glycerin in the skin toner. The hand-held wand had detected the glycerin as the explosive material. After a moment of panic, a brief conversation, and more explanation, I was cleared and sent on my way.

"Okay. No problem. You better run. You've got ten more minutes to get to your plane."

I ran back through security, had my ticket again scanned at the gate, and reboarded the airplane in time to catch my flight. By this time, I felt like I should be on a first name basis and exchanging Christmas cards with the gate agent. I passed the CBS team for a third time. They smiled at me and nodded, their questions still unanswered, and I made my way to my seat. Upon arrival at D/FW, I finally got to share the story and my brush with danger as a "suspected terrorist."

"What happened? Why were you pulled off the flight?"

I spared them the details.

"They thought I had explosive materials in my suitcase. I straightened them out. We're good!"

Just when I thought things couldn't become more comical, I soon came to learn that my car sat idle in the parking lot with a dead battery. Something inside of me has always craved the adventure of my profession. I'd just prefer that it wasn't in the form of "explosive materials." Not to worry. Reality kept me grounded. I was firmly thrust back into my world with more mundane problems to conquer.

5017 Byers Avenue - 2012

"Sold - The Final Chapter"

I turned the key in the lock for the last time, rotating clockwise, and heard the locking mechanism engage, sounding both resonant and hollow. The time had come to shutter the windows, to embrace a slower pace and move towards retirement. My life had gone another direction, and I felt confident of my decision. Yet, I was left with an indescribable emptiness. The small home on Byers Avenue was my identity, my livelihood, but most of all my dream that I had fulfilled. As my life evolved through different phases, the studio was always my constant.

I reminisced about my Grandma Mary, firm in her words, about independence and financial security.

The realtor described the property as "unique." It would sell to the right buyer. Because of the location bridging the residential homes and the commercial properties, the new owner would have flexibility. The sale of the property would allow me to downsize and eventually make my way back to Colorado, and Shannon would begin college.

I walked through the vacant building and heard my footsteps echo against the glass windowpanes. Only nail holes remained in the walls where portraits once hung. There was no need to clean; demolition would begin first thing the next morning, and the building would be gutted. Another entrepreneur would continue his journey to fulfill his dream and build his career. I would no longer need to reinvent myself through economic recessions, repaint with the changing color palette of the times, or have the roof replaced after a brutal Fort Worth hailstorm.

As I pulled the door closed for the last time, after thirty-one years as a small business owner, a wave of emotions hit me like an undulating tide, evoking many fond memories. Shannon honed her rollerblading skills in the circular drive where Ms. Texas' car once parked. Many Sundays were spent cleaning the studio while she sat in the makeup chair and face-painted herself with glee. The refrigerator and pantry were stocked with her favorite snacks, and when it was time to wind down, I would find her in my office with a pillow and blanket in front of the television.

The talent show was the highlight of the school year, when I primped four exuberant kindergarten girls at the studio for "Grease." The following year, Cindy Lauper's "Girls Just Want to Have Fun" danced through my mind. A gaggle of excited six-year-old girls in pink, leopard print skirts and coordinating scrunchies sang at the top of their lungs, while each patiently waited to have their makeup done in the coveted makeup chair.

In the early stages of the airbrush, I sprayed on temporary tattoos at the first-grade sleepover, the first night away from home for many of the young girls. High school prom reverberated through my memory, as I relived airbrushing six high school seniors for their biggest night of the school year. Even in Texas, the night air was crisp as we finished up and raced to the museum to take photos before the dance.

But largely my memories were the hundreds if not thousands of young and old women alike, debutantes, brides, pageant contestants, and mother-daughter teams who came to me for my artistry. I smiled, knowing that I had left my mark on Fort Worth and changed women's lives.

I left a box of canned cat food to entice the local feral cat that I had taken care of, placed the house key under the doormat, and walked to my vehicle. Sitting in the front seat of my silver Lexus SUV, I sobbed, unable to drive at that moment and feeling as though I were grieving the loss of a loved one. The sale of the building was emotionally tied to my decision, and it's not always easy to make the best decisions under those circumstances. Should I have sold my house and kept the studio as my new residence? Could I survive another recession? What about all of my pets? Would I be able to manage them in a new setting?

After wrestling with all of the moving pieces, I was relieved to sell and quickly cleared all of my debt from the sale of the building. It was cathartic writing checks, one after another, to release and purge the stress from my life. I was ready to move on, safely tucked away in my home. What I did not anticipate was the blow that was yet to come. Buyers, sellers, and banks were all trying to close their books. The sale of the property prior to the close of the year required a new financial statement to the colleges. What was hoped to be a renewal of my financial picture meant that Shannon was no longer eligible for a four-year scholarship.

If I had waited to close until after the first of the year, just a few short days, she would have qualified. Looking back, the clarity of decisions seems simple, but when you're in the middle of it, it's not as simple as it seems. It was a decision based on survival.

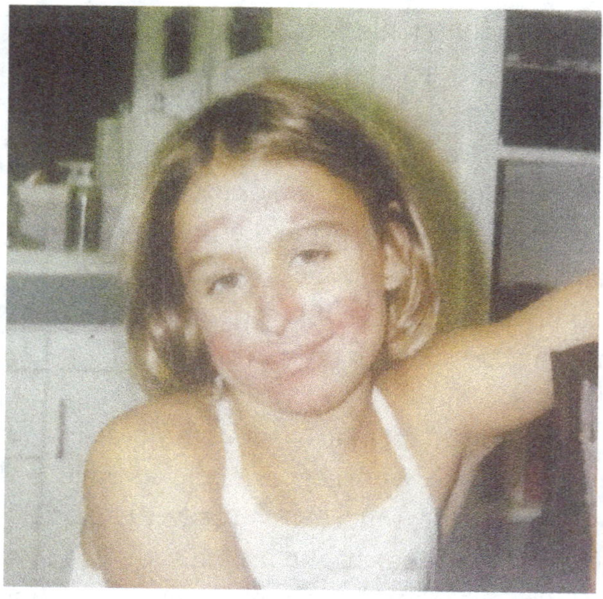

Shannon did not have her sights set on makeup.

It would be six years before I would move back to Colorado, feeling as though my thirty-five years in Texas was another lifetime, only a distant memory. I am surrounded by family, renewing old friendships and creating new ones. My daughter has now finished law school and is a practicing attorney in Colorado, on a journey to fulfill her own dream.

I am not a wealthy person, but I have lived a very rich life. I have dined with celebrities, traveled to foreign lands, and watched history unfold before me. I have created a business in my image, established many personal and professional relationships, and touched many lives. It has been a journey that I would not trade for anything, and I lived it *"Through These Eyes."*

Dan Rather
Rather Documentary Part II - 2021
"Full Circle"

It seems only fitting that my career should end where it began, full circle—my final encounter with my dear friends, Dan Rather and Wayne Nelson. We were getting close to conclusion, my sister and I, on the final chapters of the book. We were on a Zoom call, she in California, and I in Colorado. It was April of 2021, now over thirty years since my first job with CBS. The screen lit up on my cell phone, and I had received a text. "Hi, this is Wayne. Give me a call."

"Wayne?" I said to my sister, questioning the unknown caller.

"It's spam. Block the call."

"I only know one Wayne. It's his profile picture in my contacts. It's Wayne Nelson from CBS. *1-800-Serendipity,* I thought. "Let me take this call."

I immediately returned the call, hoping it was not bad news. It had been years since I last spoke with Wayne. My overactive imagination could only jump to one conclusion.

"Wow, this is a blast from the past!"

And so it began, the final chapter, literally and figuratively. A documentary, *Rather, Part II* was to be filmed in Austin, Texas, on Thursday of the following week, celebrating Dan's life and career in the broadcasting industry. I was deeply touched to be included. The cadre of three, back together for a final hurrah.

I looked out onto my patio at the six inches of newly fallen Colorado snow. My windchime swayed in the cold, bitter wind. The grass courtyard was a sea of snowdrifts against the blonde brick. How timely it would be to see the landscape of Austin, green and lush this time of year. It was a stark contrast to the icicles hanging precariously from the eaves.

I had not traveled in four years. I had not traveled since the onset of the 2020 Covid-19 pandemic. I had not traveled through airport security with my gels and liquids in over a decade. I had not become accustomed to the updated key fobs in the hotel. In technological terms, I was a dinosaur.

I arrived in the Austin-Bergstrom International Airport, caught off guard by the vacant terminal heavily impacted by the Covid-19 travel restrictions and the pandemic that had wreaked havoc on our nation.

I found my way to the taxi stand, feeling very much like my mother in a strange airport. The oddly colored automobiles disguised as taxi cabs waited in long lines at the curbside, mourning the heavy flow of passengers that was only a distant memory. The days of old, with yellow and black checkered cabs, were long gone. Living in Texas for thirty-five years where everyone drives a car, this was foreign to me. I counted my pieces of luggage, stepped into the automobile, and gave my driver instructions to the hotel.

I sat in the downtown Hilton Hotel hot tub, watching the steam rise above the surface of the water. I stared at the skyline of Austin, resting my head on the cool tile against the back of my neck. I had checked and rechecked my laundry list of supplies, neatly organized in rows of Ziploc baggies, only to be certain I must have forgotten something.

I had received the itinerary several days before. Wayne was the organized Mary Poppins that he had always been, never missing a beat.

"1:00 p.m., LuAnn Interview."

Good Lord, I thought to myself. *My role has always been behind the camera.*

"2:00 p.m. Estimated Talent Arrival. Hair and Makeup."

Perfect. That's the part I'm good at.

"6:30 p.m. Dan Rather and LuAnn chat and reminisce."

Okay. I brought plenty of photos. Dan is the skilled journalist and interviewer. I'll follow his lead.

And so it goes, the final chapter to a very long and rewarding career. The lake house rental was selected for its serenity along the waters of the Colorado River. *1-800-Serendipity.* Floor-to-ceiling windows showcased the calming waters, with exposed roof trusses allowing every bit of light into the room. The dark, wide planks of flooring and the wainscotting on the ceiling added depth to the room. The white stonework on both the accent wall and fireplace brought the outdoors inside. The camera crew had already set up for the filming, like Santa's elves working through the night. They had chosen the dining room, with the lake as a backdrop.

I was directed to the study, with its rich burnt orange paint covering the walls. The large plantation shutters allowed me to illuminate the room, which would provide fewer surprises on the camera monitor and under bright lighting. Coincidentally, there was a large ornate mirror hung on the wall, centered over a small desk, which I could use as my workstation. Yes, I could make this work. Looking back over the years, applying makeup in dimly lit hallways, moving town cars, and helicopters, I could definitely make this work.

The nerves began to melt away. I no longer had anything to prove. I was at peace with myself, comfortable in my own skin. It was an earned friendship of thirty years. What began as trial and error so many years ago was as comfortable as an old pair of shoes. The few cosmetics that I had brought with me did not look like much to the onlooker, because I knew *exactly* what I needed for this familiar palette. I had put makeup on this face so many times, on set, on air, off camera, in the field, under stage lights, and in town cars. I would work through radio interviews and telephone conversations, having him shift the receiver to the opposite ear for me to work. His mealtime often meant during the few minutes that I had to do his makeup.

The filming began with a brief behind-the-scenes interview, preparing my workstation. The neatly lined bottles of foundation, contour, brushes, and sponges were displayed for the cameras. What people don't often see are the details; the water bottle for the airbrush, the Q-tips for finite cleanups, and the lint brush for particles that will hopefully never make their way into the camera's view.

The small, white SUV pulled into the circle drive on Rivercrest Drive and rolled to a stop. The familiar sound of the gravel against the pavement resonated through the open doors of the lake house. After the apprehension and anxiety of preparing for this reunion, it was just that. A family reunion, like going home. It had been 2013, eight years prior, since our last story, and I wasn't sure that I would ever cross paths with Dan and Wayne again.

Dan is a storyteller, a journalist, unwinding the ball of yarn with ease. He began the documentary speaking about his life, from very meager beginnings, making $75 a week, through the trials and tribulations of a strong marriage surviving a move to London and the hectic news coverage of the Vietnam years. He never lost sight of where he came from or who he was. His luck, his blessings, his fortune. He spoke of family, his children, and his grandchildren, but with the most gratitude towards his dear wife of many decades, Jean. She was his rock, his stability. He reminisced about his parents, choked up, and openly cried. The layers of the onion were peeled back; it was Dan Rather raw.

What was originally scheduled for eight hours of filming became four or five. It was a blip on the screen. The documentary was to conclude at sunset, on the dock, with Adirondack chairs placed near the water's edge. We would be making a toast, with whiskey in hand, reminiscing over photos, Dan Rather, Wayne Nelson, and me. The sun would cast pink, orange, and golden hues over the waters and the story would fade out. Like a tightly timed wedding needing to be kept to a strictly calculated schedule, we ran out of time. It was an opportunity missed.

We were winding down, and I was packing up my supplies. It was at this time that I would fulfill a promise I had made to myself. I looked back over the photos through the years and appreciated my talent and the artistry of my work. But what I knew to be true was that it would not have happened, had it not been for my association with him.

I spoke of my gratitude—his presence ensuring that I would be treated with professionalism when I was part of his team—thanking him for the exposure that would lead to working with great politicians and powerful figures, catapulting my career along the way.

We assembled for the class photo, surrounded by crew thirty years my junior, for what I expect will be the last time. I began to walk away, reminded of the things most precious in life: my daughter, my family, and meaningful friendships. As time once again repeats itself, Dan says, "I want to make sure I get a photo with just LuAnn," his parting gift to me. We posed on the driveway, fallen leaves scattered underfoot, arm-in-arm, as the day came to an end, full circle.

The lake house rental on Rivercrest Drive.

Full Circle - 2021

Epilogue
"A Love Letter to My Clients" – 2023

It is with gratitude that I write to my many clients. I am humbled by your patronage and loyalty to me over the span of thirty-five years. I have come to know you as a young woman and journeyed with you through your life events—prom, weddings, and galas. I have watched you grow from a young girl in braces, blossom into a young woman, marry your soul mate, and share moments with your daughters and grand-daughters. It was always my hope that I could bring out your inner beauty, regardless of what some may view as the "ideal." I have always wanted you to see more than what you saw in the mirror.

It is at this time that I want you to know that, as much of myself as I gave to you—love, sweat, and tears—you gave as much to me in return. I have always been driven by my passion, but you gave me purpose. When asked over and over again, "Who was the most important face you have done," the answer has always been, "The one I'm working on."

Stay true to yourself, and let your inner beauty radiate the woman you were meant to be.

LuAnn

Expressions of Gratitude

Local ratings for your Seattle broadcasts were very strong, and the positive press we've gotten because you were here will have a lasting impact.
- Executive VP, CBS Evening News

I know God has crossed our paths for a reason—and for this I am so thankful. Thank you for your insight and heartfelt "words-of-wisdom." You have been such a beautiful inspiration to me. Thank you, my friend. - Donna

At the age of forty-six, it is a great moment of reassessment, a moment for dreaming fresh dreams, a moment to appreciate all the wonderful people I've gotten to work with, people like you.
- Executive Producer, CBS News

You are a very special person and Fort Worth, Texas is very fortunate to have you here. - Elaine

I could never say thank you enough for all you've done for me this year...I feel so fortunate to have been trained by you. - Leah Kay

I wish I would have known of your talent and expertise before! I have wasted so much time and money.
- Maria

I can't begin to tell you how great I feel about myself...
my self-esteem has been greatly increased thanks to
you. - Sandra

I can't begin to thank you enough for all of your hard
work in making my "natural beauty" shine through.
You definitely have a God-given talent that is a rare
gift. - Carolyn

I can't think of no more comforting thought (sic) that
you will be her cornerstone for beauty. Use your most
artistic eye in her development. - Derrick

It is so encouraging to know that people like you still
exist. - Nancy

What you have taught me is priceless. - Lisa

Thank you for your support in making our dreams
reality and successful in all aspects of life. - Mendy

You helped me more than you will ever know. Thank
you. - Heather

You made our day even more special. - Kay

You are beautiful as much on the inside as you are on
the out. I appreciate your talents and I am grateful
for your loving spirit! You are not just a make-up
artist to me, you are my friend. - Miss Texas

It does not seem to matter to you if I had one dollar or one trillion dollars. I feel like a queen. You are a very special person. - Donna

You are truly a master of your craft. - Toni

You were so encouraging and made me feel so good about myself all week. Thank you for believing in me. - Laurel

You are a true artist, and your love of your craft shows thru. - Pat

You have helped create lasting experiences shared by each contestant. - Whitnie

Thanks to your help I'm now beginning to understand the art behind make-up. - Miss Oklahoma

What an honor to work with you. - Miss Montana

It is the generosity of businesses like your studio that makes our state pageant one of the best. - Jo

You are a credit to your profession. - Joe

Thank you for bringing out the "best" of me. - Miss Missouri

Thank you and your staff so much for the support you gave to me...You helped me to feel so confident. - Nilde

You have shared a gift that she will enjoy and appreciate for a lifetime. - Faye

And thank you again—for everything. Courage, Dan

The entire CBS organization is indebted to you for your exemplary work in China. You raised the standards of our work to a new level.

On the Cutting Room Floor

"Outtakes"

"My husband says I poo like a gerbil," she said to me, in a hushed voice. "I need you to do something for me."

We were at the Hilton Anatole in Dallas, Texas. More specifically, the penthouse of the 4-Star Hotel. She was "the girl next door," with a radiant smile. It had been a long day, a full day of promotions, beginning at 6:00 a.m. There were speaking engagements and live coverage. Surrounded by executives, press, and crew coming and going, we had a moment of downtime, and we were standing in the hallway by the bathroom.

"My husband says I poo like a gerbil," she said to me, in a hushed voice. "I need you to do something for me."

"Okay, what?"

"It will be FAST. I'll get in and I'll get out, but I need for you to step into the bathroom behind me." She didn't finish the sentence. I hesitated before responding.

At first, I wasn't sure what she was asking of me. Then I understood. She wanted me to step into the bathroom immediately after her, after she had used the facilities, and spare her the embarrassment of being followed into the bathroom by someone of importance, a celebrity, or worse yet, a tabloid journalist.

I kind of smiled. I thought about what her life must have been like and felt empathy for her, always under the microscope. I stood in line for the restroom, waiting my turn.

He entered the room, already pressed for time. Seated in the makeup chair, he waited for me to begin my work. I looked at his hair, greased down and parted like the character Spanky from *Little Rascals*. The crew began to scatter, trying not to snicker. Somebody was in trouble, and it was me!

"What did you do? What is in your hair?"

"You told me to put hair gel into it."

"How much did you use? Did you use the whole tube?"

"Two minutes to air!" I heard in the distance.

And if ever there was a time for quick thinking, this was it. With a spray bottle and no shampoo in hand, the show must go on.

The Me Too movement has been going on from the beginning of time; it just didn't have a name. He sat in the makeup chair waiting to have his makeup done before going onto location. The black, vinyl cape was draped over his body, and I was standing within a few feet of him, with a female colleague on my right. I was hired as a private contractor. Because I was hired by the network, I was expected to do makeup for any other correspondents.

He brazenly sat back in the tall chair, his presence imposing in his expensive suit, starched shirt, and silk tie. As I readied myself to begin applying his makeup, he reached down, unbuckled his belt with bravado, and unzipped his trousers with a flourish.

My colleague and I looked at each other, dumbfounded and caught off guard. He was looking for shock value. We were not amused, yet because we were not alone to defend ourselves, neither of us felt intimidated.

"Stop that! Put that away! We're here to work!"

And so, he did.

Acknowledgements

Writing a book is no easy task. It has been a life-long dream to put my story onto paper. When my memory fades or I am long gone, it will be a lasting testament to my time here on Earth.

I want to thank my sister, my coauthor, for having the patience and tenacity to see it through. It was a labor of love for over three years. This would not have happened, had it not been for her painstaking, meticulous, and thorough attention to detail and hours of research. Her love for me and understanding of my idiosyncrasies captured my thoughts and expressed them with both sincerity and humor.

LuAnn